# The
# Amateur Finisher's
# Guidebook

# The Amateur Finisher's Guidebook

### BY BORDEN HALL

Gramercy Publishing Company • New York

# Contents

CONTENTS

# The
# Amateur Finisher's
# Guidebook

# ( I )

## *Yes, I Did It Myself!*

JOHN and Mary, the newlyweds, had a lot of plans for the old house they had bought and the antique furniture that was going into it. However, like many other young folks caught in the vise of high costs, they thought they would have to postpone re-decoration, not only of rooms but of furniture as well. Estimates looked pretty forbidding. It was going to cost thirty-five dollars each to refinish their several old chests and tables, to say nothing of the eleven-hundred-dollar estimate for the rooms and the floors. It looked as though they would have to resign themselves to living with dull and unattractive things until the budget could be improved. That 1940 dollar had apparently disappeared forever.

Had they not visited the apartment of their friends, the Joneses, John and Mary might have gone for years living in an environ-ment that had no right to exist in these days of modern finishes. Bill Jones told John how easy it was to do such things without professional help. The cost of materials was low, success was guaranteed and really there was an element of fun in the business. There was a certain satisfaction, Bill said, in knowing that you could accomplish such charming results and that you were really smarter than you thought you were.

Most important of all, however, was the professional appear-ance of the work, admittedly impossible a few years back with the old-fashioned materials then in use. Scientific research has brought the paint industry a long way in a short time. Aside

FIG. 1

An amateur-wrought transformation on a three-dollar chest from a second-hand store. The new miracle finishes for furniture make such useful transformation easily possible for people without previous experience.

FIG. 2

This little desk was discovered in a secondhand store and rejuvenated at a cost of approximately $1.00. Total cost $6.00.

from an improvement in quality there has also been great improvement in ease of application. No longer does the amateur need to worry about the tell-tale brush marks of a beginner. The new enamels spread and flow so flawlessly that the difference between professional and amateur application is limited to speed of application. The rules for the success of amateurs have not only been reduced in number but also made far less difficult.

But the amateur refinisher and decorator should take care in choosing his materials. It is best to stick by one good manufacturer and use his products exclusively. This will not only guarantee the best possible results but it also has an element of fairness in it. There is no absolute unity of formulas among paint manufacturers. Therefore, when we mix the products of X company with those of XX, the results may be precarious or even fatal. The lasting qualities of the paint or varnish may suffer, the color of an enamel may be affected, adhesion may be poor or checking may develop within a short time. The products of both manufacturers may be good, but when used together they may produce results that are wholly unsatisfactory. Who is going to be blamed, aside from the person who did the mixing?

Every paint manufacturer worthy of the name directs his research to produce a certain unity of product. Certain things are designed to be mixed with other things on the basis of sound chemistry or physical science. The accidental result is ruled out as far as possible. Things are designed to be foolproof. Hence we cannot too strongly recommend that we make a choice and stick to it right down the line. As an example, the writer has always stuck to Sherwin-Williams. That does not mean that they are the sole occupants of the pinnacle of perfection. Doubtless they share it with others, but it is known that their product is excellent, guaranteed and in good distribution. Even small-town dealers carry the complete line, which is highly advantageous.

Now, there are certain other requirements for good work. One of them is patience. Miraculous as the new products are, they

Fig. 3

A modern-type unfinished desk finished with one of the fast-drying enamels in pastel shade.

can be applied and made shoddy in appearance. Naturally, people living in dull surroundings are impatient to have them brightened up, and friend wife objects to the dislocations and disruptions created by redecorating. Yet these petty annoyances will have to be endured if a disastrous speed-up, a pell-mell rush to get things done is to be avoided. The results can only be bad. Better a few more days of untidiness than rooms or furniture of which we cannot be proud. In planning work of this sort, it is best not to place any time limit on it. We resolve to work until a good job is done. Besides, as amateurs, we do not know how long it may take. Professionals can estimate almost to the hour but the amateur had best refrain from such predictions.

There is one more precaution for the beginner. Let us stop to read the directions on the label even though the print is small. Satisfaction with any manufacturer's product depends upon the most intelligent use of that product. The people who know most about intelligent use are the people who made the product. Many hours of painstaking thought, many conferences with technical departments are behind the information on the label. It is precise, boiled down and results from wide experience gained in tests that may have run over a long period of months or years. Those among us who ignore or merely glance at labels are running risks that need not be run. To put it bluntly, we are being just a little stupid.

If, along with good products and patience, the amateur will use good brushes, pay attention to dust and apply the techniques to be found in the following pages, he can do fine work at great savings. After a bit of experience, confidence will come swiftly and surely and with it that glow of satisfaction and pride that always follows the remark, "Yes, I did it myself!"

# ( II )

## Brushes: How to Buy, Use and Care for Them

THIS chapter is dedicated to those benighted souls who think that a brush is just a brush and that anything that will carry paint, enamel or varnish to a job and distribute it over the surface is quite good enough. The result of such erroneous thinking is a seventy-five-cent brush that should have cost two or three dollars and a job of finishing or refinishing that will not measure up. More than that, the brush, even though cared for according to the rules, will not last and even with its first use may start to drop its bristles, always a pleasant task for a beginner to face. Better by far to have two good brushes than a half-dozen cheap ones.

The painter is just as fussy about his brushes as the carpenter is about his planes and his chisels. You can never make a mistake over an investment in a good brush, the best in fact that money can buy. It will last longer, make your work easier and make it look better.

You will want a brush made from hog bristles imported from China if possible. If not available, then the next best thing. Brushes made up of Chinese hog bristles have maximum spring (when a painter buys a brush watch him press its bristles on the back of his hand to test spring and elasticity) and each bristle has what is known as a flag end. This means that the bristle is split at the end and feathered out, which permits it to carry more paint. Such bristles also assist in a more even distribution of paint.

7

Some brushes have a mixture of long and short bristles (a small percentage of the latter) to prevent paint or enamel from running down the handle when a ceiling is being covered.

Practically all good brushes are set in rubber with excellent,

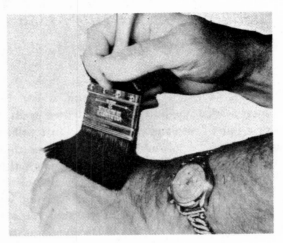

FIG. 4

Painters always test a brush for "spring" before purchase.

well-balanced handles and well-filled ferrules or upper metal sections between the handle and the bristles.

Cheaper brushes may not only have synthetic bristles but they may also be made of horsehair, a poor substitute for the true hog bristle.

Nor do we just buy a brush. It is quite true that *a* brush may be used to apply anything in any place, paint on a cellar floor, enamel on a kitchen wall or varnish on a table, but if we can afford it, we should try to have a good set of brushes, one for each type of painting or varnishing we may do. For instance, a varnish brush, if it is to produce proper flow, should have a chisel edge, and we will not need a brush of the size used for a floor if we plan to varnish only a few tables, chairs or chests. This may amount to the difference between a two-inch and a four-inch brush.

For wall painting, a painter will demand a special wall brush

Fig. 5

A few of the common types of brushes, including long and short bristle, sash and oval brushes.

with *long* bristles that will hold more paint and thereby make fewer trips to the paint can necessary. This tends to speed up the work. Such longer brushes also have longer life.

There are many types and sizes of brushes. There is the sash brush (for windows), oval varnish brushes, calcimine brushes, oval paint brushes, round brushes, Fitch flowing brushes, etc.

However, if we will tell the paint dealer exactly what we propose to do with a brush and what sort of materials we are going to apply, he will tell what to buy. We simply make sure that the quality is of the best.

Before any new brush is used, a painter usually strikes it over a board or the edge of a bench several times to dislodge loose bristles. He may thereafter wash it in turpentine or clear (untreated) gasoline to relieve it of any dust it has accumulated on the counter of the paint shop. Most brushes now come covered with wax paper, but especially in the case of varnish brushes, this should not be trusted too much and washing in clean turpentine or gasoline should still be followed out.

Further to coax any loose bristles (again, especially in the case of the varnish brush) we should (while the brush is still wet) brush it over a rough surface, such as an untrimmed board, which will tend to catch loose bristles and pull them out.

To a painter or amateur refinisher, there is nothing more exasperating than a brush that is constantly shedding its bristles. And let us make no mistake about it, cheap brushes will do it from the first to the last day of their use. If they do, there is nothing we can do about the matter except to take time out, cuss a bit and remove the detached bristle.

Let us not be so naïve as to think that we can restore an old brush encased in hard paint or varnish to a point where it can be used in a fussy varnish job or for applying a faultless coat of enamel to a breakfast-room table.

True, we have brush cleaners of all sorts whose manufacturers may make some pretty fancy claims. No doubt these cleaners will remove paint from old brushes and restore them to a usable point but not for the purposes mentioned above. Such brushes might again be used for painting the cellar stairs or floor, the outside flower boxes or the floor of the porch, but for use on furniture, inside floor varnishing or other jobs where perfection is required, never.

No matter how fussy or painstaking we may be in restoring brushes in this manner, we will find it impossible completely to remove from the bristles of such brushes the small particles of paint or varnish left from the last job. Many such particles will remain to plague us, and once they attach themselves to freshly spread varnish or enamel the problem of removing them becomes hopeless. Yes, we may wipe the paint or varnish away and make a fresh start but the particles will also make a fresh start.

This is not completely to discount the use and value of such brush cleaners. They can be valuable in restoring brushes for service in certain work. It is simply pointed out that such brushes can never be made absolutely clean.

The careful painter so cares for his brushes that he never permits them to get in such shape that they will need such drastic but not-too-good rehabilitation. Brushes should be properly cleaned and stored away with dust-proof wrappings each time we are finished with them. So treated, a brush will last for many years and render excellent service. However, once we permit paint, enamel, varnish or lacquer even partially to harden in a brush, the cleaning process will leave tiny particles that will remain indefinitely. Such particles can be so small as to be almost invisible and still cause trouble when they are deposited on a freshly covered surface.

When we are unable to finish a job of varnishing in a day, we place the brush in what is known as a "keeper." This is simply a container filled with equal parts of raw linseed oil and turpentine or Exolvent alone. Let us, for heaven's sakes, not merely place it in a can of water and leave it there for several days resting on its bristles!

Even in the prescribed solutions mentioned above, the brush should be hung by means of its handle so that no pressure will be placed on its bristles.

What about untreated gasoline? For varnish or lacquer, never. It can be used for house paint and enamel but it is not recommended. It is not too good for the bristles of an expensive brush and then there is always the danger of fire from fumes and toxic effects from inhalation.

After a brush is removed from an approved keeper solution,

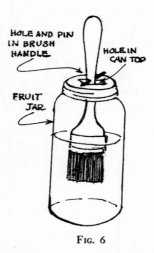

HOLE AND PIN IN BRUSH HANDLE

HOLE IN CAN TOP

FRUIT JAR

FIG. 6

A simple brush keeper for use between jobs. The brush is kept immersed in Exolvent or turpentine. Brushes should be swished out and wiped with a clean cloth before use.

like a mixture of linseed oil and turpentine, it should be thoroughly washed out in clean turpentine or Exolvent thereafter. After being swished out a few times and dried with a clean cloth it may be placed back in service immediately.

As soon as a painter has finished a job, he sets about cleaning up his brushes before the paint, varnish or enamel has a chance to begin setting up. That should be the plan of any amateur.

Cleaning is done in turpentine or other approved manufactured cleaner. First we immerse the brush and work it around to remove as much paint or varnish as possible. We then swish the brush out as violently as possible and immerse it again in clean solvent. Again we swish it out. This is followed by a good hand washing in warm water and ivory soap. Plenty of rinsing and swishing in clean warm water follows. This is followed in turn by wiping away as much water as possible with a clean rag, working down into the bristles as much as we can.

Now the brush is placed away in a clean drawer or dust-free closet for several days until the bristles are thoroughly dried out. The bristles should then be wrapped in waxed paper and a rubber band snapped around the upper end. Months or even years later we can return to such a brush feeling that it will render a service just as good as it rendered the first day it was used.

# ( III )

## Getting the Right Color

OUR favorite manufacturer of paint, much as he would like to, cannot supply his enamels or paints in a complete or even a wide range of colors or shades. If he was to do this, costs would rise sharply and he would have to charge you much more for what you get. Dealers would have to quadruple their stock, add to the size of their establishments and business would be much more difficult to conduct.

However, no manufacturer of paints or enamels asks you to limit your color tastes to the range he has selected even though you will find that the colors and shades produced are selected with great care and are suitable for most uses just as they come from the can.

If we wish shades or colors outside the available range, we will find that the manufacturer has made arrangements to accommodate us. For instance, the shades of standard Kem-Tone colors may be altered to any degree by the Kem-Tone Vogue Colors supplied in a wide range of colors and coming in half-pint cans.

The same holds for Kem-Glo, the shades of which may be changed to suit us by the addition of Fluid Tinting Colors.

In the case of oil-base paints or enamels, colors ground in oil may be used to arrive at any shade we may wish. Such colors are available in paint stores, coming in small collapsible tubes a little larger than those in which ordinary artist's colors are supplied.

This color-changing business can be very simple or very complicated, depending upon how we go about it. If we are not careful we might become so confused that one end of a table or even a room will be darker or lighter than the other end or noticeable streaks of deeper or lighter shades will develop as we go along.

These disasters—and they can be disasters—are easily preventable. We simply failed to do our mixing scientifically. This is one part of our business where we *must* keep score. For instance, we add a bit of color to a can of Kem-Glo (we are "doing" the kitchen) and we get just the right shade. Friend wife nods her full approval and we proceed to lay it on, happy in the thought that everyone is pleased. But have we forgotten that from two to three quarts of Kem-Glo might be used? Perhaps we have, so we proceed to use up the can of the right shade and then we wonder. Now was it four or six level teaspoonfuls of the color mixture we added? Jeepers! Friend wife is called in. She has forgotten, too. What a pickle!

Things might have been much less troublesome if we had used exact measurements and kept an accurate record of what was added. Then each can of the Kem-Glo could have been treated in precisely the same manner.

Another thing: when any color is added to any kind of paint or enamel, we must learn to stir and stir and stir until we are positive that the mixture is completely uniform. This cannot be overemphasized. We can stir and run, so to speak, but let's not blame the manufacturer of our paint or enamel if we do.

Perhaps we have already learned that the three so-called primary colors are red, yellow and blue. When used with black and white, all other colors and shades can be produced with these colors. Neither black or white, however, is considered a color. Mixing any two of the above-mentioned primary colors produces a secondary color. Inasmuch as there are only three primary colors there are only three secondary colors. For instance, red with yellow makes orange, red with blue makes violet and yellow with blue makes green.

In the case of true orange, it is necessary to use five parts of red to three of yellow. Variation here may make the results range from orange to poppy, scarlet, etc.

Green mixed with orange forms a tertiary color like citrine. Mixed with violet, a russet shade is created, etc.

True green is supposed to be mixed from three parts of yellow to eight of blue. When this is mixed with violet it creates olive.

Violet results when red and blue are mixed in the proportion of five of red to eight of blue.

The addition of white naturally reduces the intensity of all of the colors until the light or pastel shades are produced.

If we wish to arrive at new colors or shades by the addition of coloring mixtures supplied by the manufacturers of the material we are using, the following table will help. Perhaps in place of trying to make additions to a pastel shade (making it darker, for instance), it might be more advisable to purchase white of the same brand and add color. At any rate, some guidance in color changes can be had below:

*Blue*—Add Prussian blue to white in quantity needed to satisfy.

*Blue, delft*—Cobalt blue four parts, lampblack one part and ten parts white.

*Blue Gray*—Chrome yellow two parts, Prussian blue one part, white six parts.

*Blue Green*—White four parts, chrome green one part and Prussian blue by small amounts until satisfied with shade.

*Brown*—Light shade made with burnt umber in enough white to suit.

*Buff*—Raw sienna and white.

*Cinnamon*—Ochre, one, raw sienna two, white three parts.

*Coral*—Chrome yellow four parts, vermilion one part, white six parts.

*Cream*—Raw sienna one part and white four to six parts.

*Fawn*—Yellow ochre and burnt umber each one part, with four parts white.

*Gray, ordinary*—Lampblack in white to required depth.

*Gray, French*—Prussian blue one part, lampblack one part, white ten parts.

*Green, apple*—Chrome green one part, light chrome green two parts, white four parts.

*Green, chrome*—Chrome green one part, white one part.

*Green, grayish*—Chrome green one part, chrome yellow three parts, Venetian red one part and white ten parts.

*Green, Jade*—Chrome yellow three parts, light chrome green one part, white six parts.

*Green, Nile*—Prussian blue one part, emerald green three parts, white ten parts.

*Green, Sea*—Dark chrome green one part, white four to five parts.

*Ivory*—Vermilion one part, raw sienna three parts, white twelve parts.

*Lavender*—Madder lake, one part, ultramarine blue three parts, white ten parts.

*Lilac*—Madder lake one part, ultramarine blue one part, white twelve parts.

*Maroon*—Lampblack one part, Venetian red four parts, Prussian blue one part, white ten parts.

*Mauve*—Cobalt blue one part, Rose lake three parts, lampblack one part, white ten parts.

*Old Rose*—Crimson madder one part, white six parts.

*Orange Yellow*—Vermilion one part, chrome yellow one part, white six parts.

*Orchid*—Rose pink one part, ultramarine blue one part, white ten parts.

*Peach*—Vermilion one part, chrome yellow three parts, white six parts.

*Red, brick*—Indian red one part, Venetian red two parts, white two parts.

*Rose*—Rose lake one part, vermilion one part, white six parts.

*Salmon*—Prussian blue one part, chrome orange four parts, white six parts.

*Silver Gray*—Raw umber one part, lampblack one part, white six parts.

*Tan* —Burnt umber one part, white four parts.

*Topaz*—Vermilion one part, chrome yellow four parts, white six parts.

*Yellow Green*—Chrome yellow one part, chrome green four parts, white four parts.

Let's not accept the above directions as limiting the number of shades or colors that can be had. We will find listed here only a few of the standard mixtures. Color and shade are infinite in variety and any great extension of the subject would be subtle and confusing. However, if you wish to use the above directions as a guide, you may with patience arrive at any shade you desire. But you must be accurate and record what you do if you wish to duplicate accurately *what* you did.

Whereas color variations with Kem-Tone are produced by the addition of Kem-Tone Vogue Deep Colors, color variations in Super Kem-Tone are produced by mixing the various standard colors with each other. By such manipulation some 139 definite shades can be produced. A color guide showing each shade produced and the method of mixing for each shade will be found available at all dealers for Kem-Tone and Super Kem-Tone. As an instance, a beautiful cast of gray-green (color #25) is produced by adding one quart of Melodie Green to one gallon of Glenwood Gray. A blue green is produced (Color #48) by adding one quart Wedgewood Blue to one quart Pinehurst Green. All in all, the fussiest person will doubtless find a happy color in the 139 shades made possible by mixing standard shelf-stock colors.

Kem-Glo cannot be mixed with Kem-Tone, Super Kem-Tone or with the Vogue Deep Colors. However, the color or shade of Kem-Glo can be altered easily by the addition of Fluid Tinting

Colors carried by all Kem-Tone dealers. Thus if we wish a yellow deeper than the regular Kem-Glo yellow, we merely add yellow. If, on the other hand, we wish to lighten the shade of the regular yellow, we add Kem-Glo white. Still more to broaden the field, we may start with Kem-Glo white and add any of the tinting colors to this. The whole matter of color is very flexible nowadays and there is no need for us settling for anything but the exact shade we wish to have.

# ( IV )

## Removing Paint and Varnish

UNCLE BILL, the old tightwad, told John that there was no need of wasting money for those "fancy paint removers" when everyone had a can of lye around the house and a piece of broken glass for a scraper. Fortunately, a neighbor who knew something about refinishing furniture warned John against such a dangerous procedure.

For one thing, hot lye is an exceedingly corrosive substance that can do not only great harm to flesh and clothes but also to the wood upon which it is used. It will indeed remove old paint and varnish with a vengeance, but a single drop of it flipped from a brush can also remove the sight of an eye or cause a painful flesh burn. When such a corrosive substance reaches the wood beneath the varnish or paint, it does great damage to the wood fibers, making them soft and spongy and permanently changing the color of the wood. All considered, lye permits no economy. Any thought of its use should be ruled out.

Rather we turn to the modern chemical paint and varnish removers like Taxite involving the highly volatile solvents. While certain precautions must be exercised with these new materials, they do not offer the dangers that are offered by hot lye. Most such solvents can become toxic when inhaled over too long a period, they are highly inflammable and they dissolve fatty matter out of the skin upon contact. The restrictions then, are perfectly obvious. We never use such removers in closed rooms, we never smoke while using them or have an open flame about and we try to avoid contact with them as much as possible where the flesh is concerned.

In the latter case, that does not mean that slight contact even repeatedly—is dangerous. The skin will simply become dry and hard.

Because of the high fluidity of these solvent removers, some precaution will have to be taken to prevent running and staining of surfaces that are to be left in the open wood. Reference is made to such things as drawers in tables, chests and stands. If these are not removed and carefully treated separately, the solvent, after it picks up some of the paint or varnish to be removed, will run or seep down into the crevices between the drawers and the front of the chest and stain the open wood in the sides of the drawers in such a manner that removal will be difficult. All but the sloppiest workers try to avoid such little tragedies and they can be avoided with simple precautions.

It is also usual to remove all hardware and drawer pulls even though they are wooden. A good job of paint or varnish removal calls for getting right down to the wood at all points. This cannot be done by removing the paint around things rather than by removing the things themselves.

A great deal of sloppy work in paint and varnish removal results from a too free use of the solvents. Some amateurs erroneously think that the more solvent one puts on the faster the paint or the varnish will come off. Hence they flood a surface until the remover runs "every which way." Solvents work just so fast and no faster. What is more, we will in all probability have to put on several applications in any event. There is little or no hope of getting right down to the wood with the first application or even the second one if we are dealing with three or four layers of very old paint that is very, very hard. The paint people would be happy to give you a miracle remover of this kind but they have not been able to develop one and probably never will.

Oftentimes the seepage of solvent removers may be prevented from reaching places where they will stain open wood by the use of masking tape. For instance, when we are removing varnish from drawer fronts, it will help if we will place a piece of such

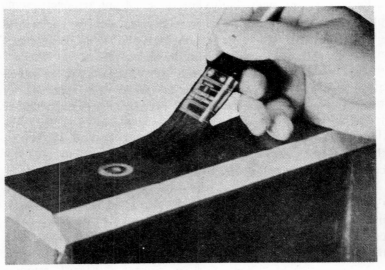

FIG. 7

Masking tape used on edges as shown will prevent varnish removers from staining open wood adjacent to surfaces being treated.

tape on either side so that should a small amount of the remover run over the edge it will not contact the open wood of the drawer sides.

When we are working with furniture, it is always best to apply the solvent to a horizontal surface, so that it will not run off edges, etc. When such solvents are placed on perpendicular surfaces, they tend to run down because of their great fluidity. In such cases, the solvent is put on in very small amounts and for a larger number of times. Otherwise, the paint or varnish at the bottom will be removed before the paint at the top is ready for complete removal.

In such cases it is best perhaps to use a paste remover which will permit uniform softening and removal.

It is usually stated on the containers of all removers that ten

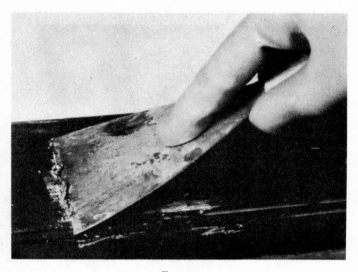

FIG. 8

A broad putty knife will help in lifting off excess varnish when solvents are used for removal.

minutes should elapse before any attempt is made to scrape off the paint or varnish. And here scraping versus wiping will depend upon the job. If you are removing the three or four layers of very old paint, say, from a pine corner cupboard made during the early part of the nineteenth century, forget about wiping with a rag. You will be in for a long session and the use of plenty of solvent, especially after the top layer is removed and you get down to the really old stuff which is as dry and hard as flint. Nothing but a large putty knife or a regular hook-type paint remover will do here.

On the other hand, if you have an old dresser with only its original varnish on it, a few applications of remover followed by wiping with clean burlap will do the trick.

Most amateurs using modern solvent paint removers for the

FIG. 9

If a receptacle is placed beneath the legs of furniture from which varnish is being removed, the legs may be washed with repeated applications of solvent, which is caught and used over again in the interest of economy.

first time try to cover too much space with each application. Depending upon the number of coats of paint or varnish we are trying to remove, you should not try to work more than two or three square feet at a time, and in extreme cases, one square foot at a time will keep you busy. More extensive coverage simply wastes solvents because most of the liquid will evaporate before we can get around to working on the paint to be removed. Progress will be just as rapid when we work a little slower.

After all paint, varnish or enamel is removed, every precaution should be taken to eliminate every possible bit of residue left by such substances, most importantly the film of wax. Should such a covering as lacquer be placed over this wax, many days will pass before the lacquer will set up hard.

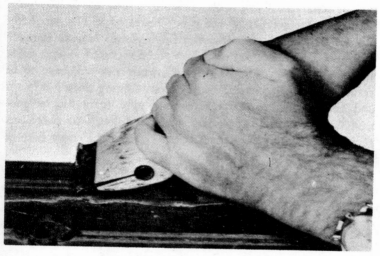

FIG. 10

Where several layers of old finish are to be removed with solvents, a hook-type scraper will greatly accelerate the job. Care should be taken to prevent the edges of the scraper from digging in.

It is usually recommended that such surfaces be washed with clean turpentine immediately after the last of the paint or varnish has been removed. However, in all cases, we simply follow the directions on the can.

Where varnish is being removed from the carved leg of a chair or table, it is best to set the leg in a can and keep bathing the leg with the solvent. Then at intervals, we pour the solvent back into the original container.

Where much old varnish is lodged in deep carvings, we simply soak it repeatedly and use an old toothbrush for removal, following this with an orange stick to pick out the remainder.

After all the varnish is removed, the job is ready for the application of abrasives and steel wool. Directions for such work are supplied in Chapter V.

In cases where several layers of very old and very hard paint are to be removed, it might be advisable to seek assistance from a steel, hook-type scraper of the type illustrated in Fig. 10. After the paint is softened, the scraper is employed to remove as much as possible. This operation may have to be repeated several times.

In using hook scrapers of this sort, beginners will have to be careful to prevent the sharp corner from digging deeply into the wood being stripped. Some extremely ugly scars can be produced in this manner and they will be difficult to patch up, especially in cases where a transparent varnish or lacquer is to be employed.

It is also necessary to keep such scrapers very sharp if they are to be effective. The angle at which they are used is also important. (See Fig. 7.) If a very hard, flintlike old paint is being removed, the scraper should be sharpened at frequent intervals, preferably on a small, fine grinding wheel.

Naturally scrapers are not recommended for anything but perfectly flat surfaces. If we attempt to use them, for instance, in removing paint from round legs, the pressure at the point of contact is apt to be so high that actual cutting into the wood will result.

Very thin coats of old, brittle varnish on flat surfaces may be removed by the use of scrapers alone if we proceed carefully and without too much pressure. If the pressure on the cutting blade of the scraper is applied uniformly, there will be no danger of the corners of the blade cutting deeply into the surface.

There are a number of types of scrapers on the market. The hook type illustrated in Fig. 7 is the most efficient cutter but it is also the most dangerous to use when in the hands of an amateur. Hence great care is needed.

# ( V )

# *The Intelligent Use of Abrasives*

YOU might just as well face the truth now: no really good job of refinishing, whether on old or new surfaces, can be done without "elbow grease" and abrasive material, most of it in the form of what we broadly call "sandpaper." Nowadays, however, sandpaper relates only to the flint-coated paper which was almost universally applied fifty years ago. Today we have wonderful new abrasives in coated forms. "Coated forms" refers to abrasives of various "grits" (size of abrasive particles used) mounted on paper by some sort of adhesive or "bond" as the trade calls such things.

Aside from ordinary sandpaper (flint, that is) we have coatings of garnet, aluminum oxide (sold under various trade names), silicon carbide (of which Carborundum is one trade name) and emery. As wood finishers and refinishers we will be interested only in flint, garnet and aluminum oxide.

Sandpaper is cheapest of all coated papers and the least durable. Garnet paper is superior and lasts longer, which might also be said of aluminum oxide. However, a good job can be done with any one of the above materials providing the correct grades are used in the proper sequence and we are not afraid of doing a bit of work. We repeat again that no ultimate surface can be better than the surface with which we start. Therefore, if a surface is not carefully prepared before the paint, varnish, lacquer or enamel is applied, we cannot expect such finishing materials to produce miracles. Our paint people would be happy to pass such things on to us but so far they have not been able to do it and we had better not put off any of our jobs waiting for such a thing to happen.

When you ask your hardware dealer for sandpaper, he will ask you what grit you want. Roughly, there are fine, medium and coarse. However, there are several degrees of fine, medium and coarse, so it is best that we learn to speak in the terms of the manufacturers who give the various grits numbers.

## TABLE OF ABRASIVE GRIT NUMBERS

| | Flint | Garnet | Al. Oxide | Carborundum |
|---|---|---|---|---|
| Very Fine | | 10/0 | 360 | |
| | | 9/0 | 320 | |
| | | 8/0 | 280 | 8/0 |
| | | 7/0 | 240 | 7/0 |
| | 4/0 | 6/0 | 220 | 6/0 |
| Fine | | 5/0 | 180 | 5/0 |
| | | 4/0 | 150 | 4/0 |
| | 3/0 | 3/0 | 120 | 3/0 |
| | 2/0 | | | |
| Medium | | 2/0 | 100 | 2/0 |
| | 1/0 | 1/0 | 80 | 0 |
| | ½ | | | |
| Coarse | | ½ | 60 | ½ |
| | 1 | 1 | 50 | 1 |
| | 1½ | 1½ | 40 | 1½ |
| | 2 | | | |
| Very Coarse | 2½ | 2 | 36 | 2 |
| | | 2½ | 30 | 2½ |
| | 3 | 3 | 24 | 3 |
| | 3½ | | | |

If we will refer to the table supplied herewith, we will note that, in the case of ordinary flint (sand) paper, the finest grade starts with 4/0 while the very coarsest is plain 3½. Naturally in working up any surface, before any form of covering is applied, we start with a rather coarse grade of paper and work up to finer grade. Much will depend upon what we are finishing, the condition of the wood, the nature of the wood, etc. It does not follow that we always start with the coarsest grade of any paper and wind up with the finest, using all of the seven or eight grades involved. It would rarely be necessary to use more than two or three grades of paper in working up a surface.

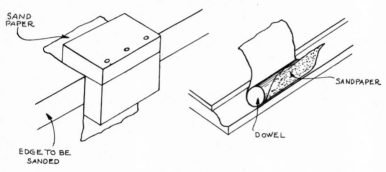

FIG. 11

A piece of dowel will assist in sanding a cyma-edge top. Left: Rounded edges of square edge can be prevented with the simple device shown.

To get the greatest cutting efficiency with such papers, it is necessary to use them with a block of wood. This equalizes pressure, whereas merely pressing such paper to the work with the fingers does not. A sanding block need not measure over 3/5 or 4/6. Perhaps the rank amateur will need to be cautioned about always sanding *with* the grain and *never* across it. Going across grain with coarse paper will leave such deep and ugly scratches as to defy ordinary removal except by heroic hard work or a plane or scraper. This is a warning.

Here is a typical procedure. If sandpaper is used, we start with $\frac{1}{2}$ grit or even coarser if the surface is in bad shape. This is used aggressively and the surface is covered as uniformly as possible. Doubtless such coarse grit will leave visible scratches, which in turn are removed with a finer grit, say 2/o. The last sanding is done with 3/o or 4/o.

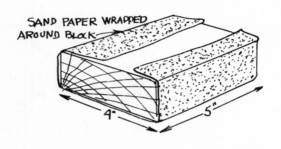

FIG. 12

A sanding block keeps even pressure on sanded surfaces, whereas the fingers produce small areas of pressure and uneven results.

But we are not finished with preparation as yet. There is still another very simple treatment that will work wonders. As a final operation, we wad up a piece of fine steel wool and rub the surface briskly with it.

After sanding of any kind, a large amount of wood flour or fine wood dust will be left in the grain of the wood. If possible every last particle of this must be removed. Otherwise, it will be picked up by our enamel or varnish and pulled out of the wood pores, leaving the enamel or varnish with anything but a perfect surface. Hence, we moisten a clean rag with turpentine or Exolvent and wipe the clean wood vigorously *with* the grain and *across* the grain.

Of course, power sanding equipment of the portable variety can be employed but there is little need for such machinery on small articles of furniture. Naturally, rotary power sanders can be fatal and only the continuous belt type should be used if they are used at all. Almost every large hardware store will now rent such machines on an hourly basis.

Aluminum oxide and other abrasive papers intended for use by hand are now available for either *dry* or *wet* use. Papers intended for wet use are oil treated so that the water or mixture of oil and water used will not soften the paper.

The object of the so-called wet paper will be perfectly clear upon a moment's reflection. Such papers are supplied only in the finer grits and intended for use with water or water-oil mixture as a lubricant that will reduce the cutting power of the abrasive material. Used without water, these papers may cut too rapidly. Used with it, they cut more slowly, thereby giving the operator better control and in the end a smoother, better job.

In building up varnish finishes, careful workers usually give the first coat of varnish such treatment as to prepare a smoother surface upon which to lay the second coat. The same holds for the application of enamel and lacquer. These procedures will be described more fully later in some of our actual instructions for refinishing.

As a parting word, let it be said that we will save a great deal of labor if we learn when to discard a piece of abrasive paper. It does not take long for ordinary paper to become plugged or clogged. The spaces between abrasive particles become jammed with wood flour or dust and gradually this builds up until the abrasive particles are partially lifted out of contact with the wood surface. Added to this, of course, the abrasive particles become dulled. Consequently, those who think that they can use a small piece of abrasive paper all evening without adding to their burden uselessly, simply do not know their abrasive papers.

# ( VI )

# On Using Bleaches

SOME day you will be faced with a wood-bleaching problem. You may wish to clean up a stained surface or, more likely still, you will wish to bleach wood in preparation for one of the marvelous new blond finishes mentioned in Chapter XIX. In any event, here's the "dope."

Bleaches may be prepared at home or purchased already mixed, although many small towns or country dealers have so little demand for such ready-mixed material that they do not stock it.

A bleach is simply a mixture of chemicals that have the power to lighten the color of certain things. The "peroxide blonde" discovered long years since that hydrogen peroxide can accommodate "gentlemen who prefer blondes." This same chemical is used in some wood-bleaching solutions. The same holds for the material sold for cleaning last year's straw hat: oxalic acid which comes in the form of white powder or crystals.

The bleaching solution, whatever it may be, is simply brushed on the wood in ample amounts and permitted to dry, after which it may be washed off or neutralized or both. If sufficient bleaching is not effected with the first application, then we continue until the surface has been lightened to a satisfactory point.

Now it so happens that there is no norm in bleaching wood. A bleach that may work wonders on walnut will be a total flop on oak or cherry. This is quite as it should be. Wood varies a great deal in chemical composition as it relates to coloring matter, and some bleaches will be better than others for certain specific uses.

Some woods, such as oak, birch, mahogany, ash, maple, beech and walnut, bleach out with ease. On the other hand, gum, pine and poplar are very difficult to handle, and there is always the question of whether or not we wish even to try to bleach white pine. Grain-wise it is a characterless wood and bleaching will certainly not improve its appearance.

It often happens that after we have removed the varnish or paint from a piece of old furniture and wish to cover it anew with clear varnish or lacquer, we may have to apply a powerful bleach to get at remaining stains. But let us not make the mistake of believ ing that a bleach can produce magic. Every speck of the wax deposit left by a paint remover must be eliminated, which is best done with a turpentine or gasoline wash and the vigorous use of sandpaper of diminishing grit so as to open the plugged grain. This gives the bleach a chance to penetrate. Otherwise, it will remain on the surface and we will be tempted in our ignorance to cuss out either the writer or the manufacturer of the bleach used. In short, before bleach is applied to such a surface we try in every way to get the wood as clean and uniform in color as possible. Inasmuch as all of these bleaches are made up of certain chemicals dissolved in water, we can understand that even the slightest film of wax will separate them from the wood completely.

And let us not make the mistake of thinking that the use of bleach can entirely replace the "elbow grease" needed to remove stains. Bleach may reduce the shade of such stains as remain, but their total removal should not be expected. Remedy? Sandpaper!

Now a word of caution. All bleaches are harmful to the skin to some degree. Bleaches containing sodium hydroxide and powerful concentrations of hydrogen peroxide are not only harmful to the skin but to the eyes as well. Hence, you are strongly advised in any case to wear a cheap pair of goggles and rubber gloves when applying such materials.

If we plan to purchase ready-mixed bleach from a large supply house, then we had better tell the salesman just what type of wood we propose to use it on. On the other hand, if we mix our own bleaching solutions, we are advised to use them on small pieces or test panels of the wood we wish to give a blond finish.

As an instance, we might try a mixture of caustic soda and

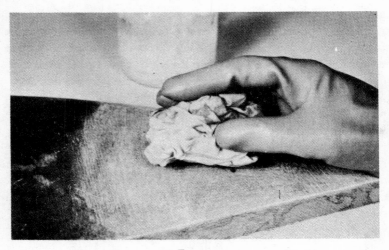

FIG. 13

Bleach is applied with rubber gloves to prevent damage to the skin.

hydrogen peroxide (as supplied at paint stores) on mahogany. One pound of caustic soda is used to one gallon of warm water. The wood upon which the mixture is used is laid horizontal so that the bleach will have an opportunity to lie long enough to act. It should be flooded on. This will not be possible on perpendicular surfaces.

It could be that we will be able to find a good bleach at the corner grocery store. Sodium hypochlorite will make most wood, save oak which it actually darkens, several shades lighter. Household laundry bleaches sold under the tradename of Linco and Clorox may be employed. This substance is also very effective for bleaching out wood discolored with water stains.

There are a number of two-chemical bleach treatments on the market. One is made up of oxalic acid and sodium bisulphite and another of sodium bisulphite and potassium permanganate. Strong active solutions of such bleaches call for 10 per cent (by weight) of each chemical mentioned in warm water. In the case of the oxalic-acid-sodium-bisulphite combination, the solution of oxalic acid is applied first with a brush and allowed to dry. This is followed by flooding on the sodium bisulphite. The crystallized residue of the oxalic acid liberates sulphur dioxide from the sodium bisulphite and this is the active bleaching agent.

With the second combination, potassium-permanganate-sodium-bisulphite, that is, the potassium permanganate is applied first. Here you must not be alarmed over the brown color produced. If you seek a very light final effect, it is best to apply several coats of potassium permanganate, allowing each one to dry out before another is applied. This brown color is quickly eliminated by the first application of sodium bisulphite solution. After the proper degree of bleaching is achieved, the wood should be carefully sponged off with clean, warm water and permitted to dry.

The two-solution bleach mentioned below is a powerful one. The solution applied first is made up of 1 lb. of caustic soda and 1 lb. of silicate of soda to 10 lbs. of water. The second solution, that is the solution that is applied *after* the first has been applied and allowed to dry, is 30 per cent hydrogen peroxide and 70 per cent water. This, too, is allowed to dry after it is applied. If the application of the hydrogen peroxide is not sufficient to produce the sort of light color demanded, then we simply continue adding the second solution until sufficient bleaching is produced.

After the correct color has been achieved, the surface is washed with a mild neutralizer in warm water, in this case acetic acid, which may be strong vinegar. This in turn is rinsed away with clean warm water.

It is fatal to apply finish of any kind over a residue of caustic. Therefore, if we have a choice piece of furniture which we have carefully bleached and with which we are fully satisfied, it is best to test the surface to make sure that it is not highly alkaline.

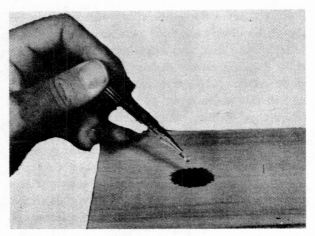

FIG. 14

Testing a surface for excessive alkalinity before finish is applied. Excessive alkalinity must be corrected with weak acetic acid, followed by flushing with clean warm water.

This is done with the following solution applied with a medicine dropper:

> 1 part phenolphthalein
> 50 parts ethyl alcohol
> 50 parts water

Drops of this solution are distributed over the bleached surface. If any spot turns red or pink after a minute or two, the surface is too dangerously alkaline for finishing. Hence, more acetic acid is applied. A residue of alkaline material will eventually cause blister and pimples to a degree that will call for complete refinishing.

After we are satisfied that the surface is chemically clean, the piece is laid away for at least forty-eight hours for *complete* drying. If this is done in a heated room, we can be sure that forty-eight hours is enough. If the weather is humid, the chances for complete drying in this period will not be sufficient. Your judgment here can be important.

It follows that the water in the bleaching solutions will raise the grain of the wood slightly. On the other hand, we must be careful about sanding lest we cut through the bleached layer of wood with sandpaper in an effort to level the grain. Perhaps it is best to use fine steel wool for this purpose. It will cut more slowly than even the finest garnet paper but fast enough for the purpose at hand.

# ( VII )

## *Brushing and Rolling It On*

BRUSHING on paint, varnish, lacquer or enamel is not quite so easy as it looks, when the job is done properly. There is a little more to it than merely dipping a brush and brushing its charge out with the grain. A great deal depends upon the medium with which we are working. We may apply too much varnish and not brush it out enough (that is, distribute it) or we may apply too little and brush it out too much. We may also work in such a way as to leave brush marks or cause weeping (running on vertical surfaces). In any event efficient use of the brush is not difficult to master. The fundamentals follow:

For one thing, practically all beginners either pick up too much or too little with the brush. Simply dipping the end of the brush in the medium and quickly brushing it out is poor practice and much too slow. A great portion of the time spent will be consumed in going back and forth between the paint can and whatever we may be working on. This is mere daubing, not painting.

The other extreme is the fellow in a terrible hurry who dips the brush almost to the ferrule and carries three times as much paint to the job as he should. It usually happens that such a worker does not stop to brush the paint out evenly, and this results in an uneven film far too thick on the whole. If varnish or certain enamels are involved, this thickness delays drying time and thereby increases trouble from dust deposits.

Of course, before any brushing is done, we must first make sure that the paint or enamel is thoroughly mixed to a uniform color. This requires patient stirring with a stick or small paddle.

Consistency will also be important. If the material is too thick to brush out easily (judged by the degree of "pull" or drag on the brush) then we should add some of whatever thinning agent is mentioned in the printed directions on the can.

Regardless of the length or nature of a brush or the medium being spread, the brush should be dipped to only one-third the length of the bristles. All excess is wiped off on the edge of the can and the brush is always carried to the work with the bristles pointing down. This prevents the load from running down into the ferrule.

And we must not grasp the brush desperately and tightly while painting. It is held in a relaxed manner and worked back and forth smoothly and easily with constant, medium pressure. There is no need of applying pressure until the bristles are bent back to the heel.

If we are painting the siding on a house, we use as long a stroke as possible, so long as the paint continues to be spread uniformly. At the end of each stroke, we lift the brush just enough to clear the surface before the reverse is started.

A good painter senses good, even distribution and never goes on brushing beyond the point where he thinks it is achieved. Usually four or five strokes back and forth is enough to bring this result.

In the case of flat surfaces, we simply brush it out until smoothness and even distribution are achieved. Anything beyond this can be positively harmful for this reason: Continued brushing tends to separate the liquid carrier from the pigment or coloring matter. Where too much of the carrier or oil is brought to the surface and dries, glossy spots will develop: islands of gloss, we might say that give the whole job a blotchy appearance. This tends also to leave brush marks except where the new wonder enamels like Kem-Glo are used.

Really the problem of brush marks is practically nonexistent with the new resin-emulsion or water-mix paints and enamels. Slight evidence of brush marks might be had when a covering like Kem-Glo is first applied but they will completely disappear within a short time. However, if the old enameling covering over which Kem-Glo is being applied has heavy brush marks on it, these will show through the new covering to some extent and nothing can be done about it. Certainly we should not be so silly as to blame Kem-Glo which, after all, in a large measure must reflect the nature of the surface over which it is applied.

In all cases, good light striking our work at the proper angle will be important. If the natural light is not good, then electric light should be arranged in a manner that will permit us to view the applied surface properly. Skilled workers do not need such assistance.

Enamel and varnish, no matter where they are being applied, are always flowed on with a fairly full brush. To achieve a fuller brush without dipping up to the ferrule, we simply refrain from wiping too much of the dip off on the edge of the can.

Starting with a fairly full brush, we first use several flowing strokes side by side and *with the grain*. After even distribution, we stroke across the grain. After that, our brush will be empty and we then use several very light passes *with* the grain again, our brush now being just about empty.

Again, it is stated that the incidence of the light on the work is important. Let's arrange lighting so that we can always see what is happening.

Where a piece of furniture is being worked upon with varnish, enamel or lacquer, matters will be greatly simplified if we turn the piece so that we are always working on a horizontal surface. Such surfaces will permit better lighting. Then, too, if amateur-like, we do apply too much material, no weeping will result if we leave each surface in a horizontal position long enough for a "set" that will just prevent weeping. With the modern enamels or with lacquer, this does not need to be very long.

Indeed some of these materials set so rapidly that, once we start on a table top or the side or top of a chest, we should finish it without stopping even long enough for a phone call. Otherwise we are apt to have a visible lap. The fresh material placed over the too-tacky edge of material previously applied is very apt to "roll" it, which creates a very sad ripple effect. When an amateur does this, he is in trouble up to his ears.

Indeed in painting or varnishing surfaces, we always block off a portion that must be completed before we stop. For instance, in enameling a kitchen wall, we try to complete one whole side in one session. If we start on the ceiling, we should see to it that we have enough time at our disposal to complete it before we stop. Few painters go home with a wall or ceiling half done.

Lacquer, either clear or colored, when properly applied, produces an excellent surface—excellent for wear and for resistance to damage by chemical action from such things as water and alcohol. However, it is admittedly difficult to apply, especially for amateurs, and indeed most professional painters shy away from it whenever possible.

It is not difficult to trace the problem of lacquer to its source. The solvents used in such material are terrifically volatile, which is just another way of saying that they evaporate with great speed. This speed of evaporation of necessity calls for speed in application. The mere lapse of a few seconds or a minute makes it highly dangerous to return to a covered area to brush out an imperfection or to cover a neglected spot. The result of such tampering can be utterly disastrous. Further brushing will cause the lacquer to roll or ripple, and the only sure cure is complete removal.

However, many such tragedies can be avoided if lacquer is put on with the proper incidence of light on the surface being worked. Good lighting is most important. That with the technique described below will permit any amateur to make a fairly good job of applying lacquer.

We have already said something about the desirability of

working with horizontal surfaces wherever possible so that there will be less chance of running or weeping as the painters call it. You are especially warned of this in connection with lacquer. Thus if you are working on furniture, always turn it so that the surface being worked upon is horizontal.

We are here discussing the application of lacquer with a brush, although it is confessed that application is much easier by means of spraying.

Surfaces to which lacquer is to be applied must be scrupulously free of wax or grease of any kind. A slight residue of wax left from an application of varnish remover can be fatal by delaying drying time. In such case the powerful solvents in the lacquer immediately pick up and dissolve the wax or grease, which results in a combination that may take days to harden.

And you must remember that lacquer cannot be placed over any kind of a painted, enameled or varnished surface that can be removed by the modern solvent removers. The reason is simple. The solvents used in lacquer are similar to the solvents used in paint and varnish removers. Therefore, immediately lacquer is applied, say to an enameled surface, the solvents in the lacquer go to work on the base coat and within a few minutes' time you will have a sight sorry to behold.

Of course, no matter how lacquer is applied, you are warned not to go about your work with a cigarette dangling from your lips. In the case of spray application, this can be very dangerous from a fire and explosion viewpoint. Also if you spray, it is most advisable to wear a covering over your mouth. Some people are very sensitive to the toxic effects of the solvents used in lacquers. Working out of doors is always advisable whenever possible but here we must keep out of the sunlight, the heat of which tremendously accelerates the evaporation of the solvents used in lacquers. As a matter of fact working in direct midsummer sun with any of the fast-setting modern interior finishes is not advisable.

FIG. 15

Loading a roller applicator with paint from a shallow pan. Rollers speed
application of the modern wall finishes and produce uniform application.

The brush used for the application of lacquer should not be either too soft or too coarse and stiff. Rather it should be a medium soft Fitch brush of good quality. If our paint dealer knows his business, he will probably recommend the right kind of a brush. If furniture is being worked on, the brush need not be over two inches wide. This should be of the flat varnish type set in rubber.

Lacquer should always have an undercoating, either one especially designed for use with lacquer, or a very *thin* coat of shellac. Where lacquer is being applied to new wood, a thin coat of white shellac will act both as sealer and undercoating. It is true that the solvents in the lacquer will affect the shellac but the coating should be so thin as to cause no trouble.

Really lacquer is flowed on rather than brushed. You brush lacquer as little as possible and the more you brush it, the greater the possibilities of trouble. You must never run a brush out of its lacquer supply, that is you must never brush away until the brush itself has no more to give. Keep the brush well supplied by frequent trips to the can but always wipe away the excess on the edge of the can, working as rapidly as possible.

Lacquer brushes should be held at an oblique angle rather than in a perpendicular fashion and uniformity of deposit should be controlled as much as possible by pressure on the brush. If you hesitate long enough to run the brush back and forth six or seven times before you return to the can for a fresh supply you will soon get into trouble.

Flowed on properly and in sufficient volume, we do not need to worry about brush marks when using lacquer. This material levels off beautifully.

If we are skillful enough to apply lacquer successfully as it comes from the can, we need not worry about the need for a second coat. One coat will be quite sufficient and will supply a hard surface after it has been allowed to set for forty-eight hours. Application is always easier, however, if some thinner is

FIG. 16

Applying Kem-Tone (or Super Kem-Tone) over old wall paper with a roller applicator.

used. The more thinner, the thinner the covering will be and less wear will be supplied. If thinned by as much as 50 per cent, one coat will not usually be sufficient. It is true, however, that many amateurs find it desirable to thin lacquer by adding such a high percentage of thinning liquid and then applying two or more coats, using fine wet garnet paper between applications. Experts agree that if this is done, the lacquer should be given forty-eight hours in which to set up between coats even though such applications may feel perfectly dry to the touch after the lapse of one hour. Final coats of lacquer may be treated with abrasives and waxed like other surfaces.

The mixing of paints and varnishes may sound too simple for words. As amateurs we do not know how much needless trouble we can get into if we mix air into some materials, varnish for instance. Even in pouring varnish from a can we may get too much air mixed with it. In the case of a gallon container with a spout it should be poured in such a way as to prevent gurgles. In short, it should be poured by tilting the can so gently that the varnish will flow in an even stream.

Shaking varnish cans vigorously can also entrap air and once varnish is mixed with air the painter will be troubled with tiny bubbles appearing on his work, a most exasperating experience with no ready or easy remedy. Once air becomes entrapped with varnish, it is very difficult to remove it. In stirring any mixture, we should work slowly and gently, avoiding undue agitation.

Because of the easy flowing quality of the newer wall and ceiling paints, such as Kem-Tone and Super Kem-Tone, rapid application by means of a special roller is possible. When such rollers were first introduced for such application, the old-time painters looked upon them askance. Now, however, when large spaces are to be covered, they invariably employ such devices.

These rollers simply amount to a cylinder covered with a certain fabric and mounted on a handle. The cylinder is rolled into the paint to be used and then in turn rolled over the surface to be covered. An excellent distribution of paint follows.

There is also a fountain-type of roller available. In this case, the paint is poured into the cylinder or roller, which is also covered with a special fabric. The paint soaks through this fabric sufficiently fast for distribution over the surface being covered.

Here's how ordinary rollers work. You will need a flat-bottom pan propped up at one end. Get your paint ready and pour enough into the pan to cover the lower two-thirds, leaving the upper third dry. Roll the roller down into the paint, then back out over the dry end to remove any excess. Next, roll the paint on the wall. Start about three feet below the ceiling. Roll up, then down over the same strip. When three such strips are done, go lightly across them with your roller. Like magic, you have a beautiful, uniform coat of color with subtle "textured" effect that is high fashion for all interior walls. Obviously, there is no chance for brush marks. The only time you use a brush is to paint narrow bands next to the woodwork. Do this first, so you can roll over the edges for uniformity.

The roller is six inches wide and holds much more paint than a brush and gives you much more "reach." You can cover twice the area in a single stroke, and there is no messy dripping even when you do the ceiling.

The roller can be used on all interior wall surfaces with paints like Kem-Tone, Kem-Glo, Super Kem-Tone, Flat-Tone or any other paint. After using, the roller is easy to clean with water or turpentine, depending upon the paint applied. When dry, it will be ready for the next redecorating project.

# ( VIII )

# *Water and Spirit Stains*

SPIRIT (alcohol) stains and stains mixed with certain synthetic chemicals such as Carbitol and Cellosolve can be purchased ready-mixed in most large supply houses. One such well-known stain is the Sherwin-Williams Artistain concentrates and Artistain Ready-Mixed, both of which use dyes for coloring.

The dyestuffs used in spirit and water stains can usually be purchased in dry form and in quantities as little as one ounce. However, an ounce of such material may go a long way in making enough stain to cover many articles of furniture. Expense, too, is low.

Many expert furniture finishers still prefer the use of water stains. They are easily mixed with dry powder (all other types of stains can be purchased already mixed), they can be applied with ease, they penetrate very well, etc. They do, however, have a tendency to swell, expand or raise the grain of most wood, in some cases so seriously as to call for light resanding after the stain has dried. Unless this sanding is done with a great deal of care, there will be danger of cutting through the stain, which makes for real trouble.

Before water stain is applied, it is advisable that we first sponge the surface with a reasonably wet sponge and then wipe off the excess water. This is followed by the brushing on of the stain but we must make sure before this stage is reached that we have arrived at the color we wish by means of a test panel. In making test panels it is not safe to decide finally until our panels have dried out because no matter what sort of stain we employ, it is the color when dry that will have to satisfy. Not only that but the true and final color will show only when the varnish or lacquer has been placed over the dried stain. In cases when we are going to be very fussy over final color or shade, the finishing of several test panels is highly recommended. Here, however, such testing will be without value unless we number each panel and keep a record of the concentration of each stain mixture that was used.

In speaking of depth of color we must also bear in mind that we have two factors. One is the degree of porosity and the softness of the wood with which we are dealing. As an instance, we might leave a mahogany stain on a hard, close-grained piece of wood for ten minutes before we wiped away the excess, only to find that the depth of color was not sufficient. The same stain left for five minutes on a piece of pine (which stains very poorly) might produce a color far too deep to suit us.

The other X factor is the time element. The longer *any* stain is left in contact with wood before the excess is wiped away, the greater the depth of color produced.

The problem of end grain is present no matter what kind of stain we use. End grain will suck in a large amount of water stain, thereby making end edges of table tops, etc., especially dark unless we take the precaution of diluting the stain before we apply it.

After water stain is perfectly dry (forty-eight hours usually) we can seal the surface with a shellac wash composed of one pint of white shellac to seven parts of thinner or alcohol. If we plan to use lacquer over such a surface, then we must purchase a special sealer intended to be placed beneath lacquer surfaces. These are called lacquer-sealers and some expert finishers use a stain which is miscible (spirit) with such sealers so that the sealer and the stain are applied simultaneously. However, when it comes to this sort of business, we should remember our amateur standing.

The procedure from this point onward will depend upon the

type of wood being finished. If it is a close-grained wood, we simply wait for the sealer to set hard and then go over it very gently with fine steel wool or very fine garnet paper. After this, the dust left is wiped away with a cloth moistened with turpentine. If lacquer is to be used in place of varnish, we must make doubly sure that all traces of the turpentine are either evaporated or wiped away with a clean rag before the lacquer is applied.

If we are dealing with a coarse-grained wood such as chestnut or oak, we may have to use a filler, depending upon the effect we desire. Our chapter on fillers will cover such application.

The same stains that are mixed with water and which when used with water only have a tendency to raise grain more than any other stain mixture, may be reduced to a non-grain-raising state by first, producing a highly concentrated mixture in hot water and then mixing or diluting this with Sherwin-Williams Artistain Solvent. If such a mixture is not available, then the partially dissolved water stain may be mixed with diethylene glycol (Carbitol) or ethylene glycol (Cellosolve) until the desired color concentration is reached. Such mixtures produce little or no raising of grain and therefore need no sanding after they are dry.

In mixing water stains it is usual to dissolve one ounce of the dry powder in one quart of warm water and dilute as needed when the stain is used.

True spirit stains may be purchased already mixed or they may be mixed at home. In the latter case, we add one ounce of alcohol-soluble stain powder to one quart of warm denatured alcohol, the warming being effected by immersing the alcohol container in a pan of hot water and leaving it there long enough for the alcohol to pick up sufficient heat.

We are warned that spirit stains are the most difficult of all to use. Were it not for the fact that the writer might be accused of neglecting the subject, he would not have mentioned such stains. These stains, although far more difficult to use than others because of their terrific speed of drying, still have no great advantage over water stain mixed with solvents like Carbitol and Cellosolve. If we persist in using spirit stains in alcohol, we should add one-eighth of a pint of white shellac to each quart of solution and about one cupful of naphtha. These ingredients act to retard the drying of such stains.

An excellent stain that will not raise grain in the least is made by dissolving one ounce of water-soluble stain powder in either one of the solvents previously mentioned, Cellosolve or Carbitol.

If you happen to be refinishing a piece of furniture with inlay, it will be necessary to protect this from the stain. Naturally in the preparation of surfaces having inlay, it is difficult to avoid sanding the inlay, thus opening its grain and making it ready to suck up stain. It will be necessary to carefully cover this inlay with shellac applied with a small brush. A very light coat can be applied (that is, highly diluted) and it can be left in place.

Now a few words about the various common woods and the stains that may be used with them should be helpful.

We take mahogany, for example, of which there are many kinds, some of it not mahogany at all although sold with that label. What is said about mahogany will also hold for walnut.

Both of these woods respond beautifully to bleaching procedures described in another chapter. After bleaching, the wood may be toned in any color desired with a very light stain wash. Or, if we wish to preserve the original color or produce something akin to it, we can apply tones of red or brown in ordinary concentrations. Either water or the non-grain-raising type of stain using synthetic chemical as the solvents (Carbitol or Cellosolve) should be used on these woods.

A red stain is usually used with cedar for the purpose of reducing the color contrast between the white or light and the red sections. Any type stain may be used.

Oak on the other hand may be toned or colored with any stain but the water type. Water stain will seriously raise grain on wood of this kind. Bleach may also be used most effectively on this wood, after which color toning with light stain may be done with good effect.

On the whole the woods fir, spruce, pine, basswood, cypress, poplar and redwood will work best with penetrating oil stain. Birch, gum, maple and beech should be stained with a non-grain-raising stain such as described above.

If we wish to mix our own stains of various colors and kinds the following guide to color will be helpful. This is given in units of liquid parts.

| | Yellow | Orange | Dark Blue | Red | Black |
|---|---|---|---|---|---|
| Mahogany | | 12 | 3 | 5 | |
| Golden Oak | | 22 | 4 | 2 | |
| Dark Oak | 2 | 10 | 5 | | |
| Brown Mahogany | 1 | 18 | 4 | | |
| Light Walnut | | 10 | | 1 | 4 |
| Dark Walnut | | 12 | | 1 | 6 |
| Light Oak | 1 | 10 | | 2 | |
| Maple | 4 | 10 | | 2 | |
| Red Mahogany | 2 | 10 | | 6 | 4 |

As a parting word about applying stain, let this be said: If we must err on depth of tone, let it be on the light side. When a shade is too light, we can always apply another coat of stain and wipe it away. However, when the shade is too dark, we are pretty well "stymied." Yes, we can rub it with alcohol or turpentine or apply sandpaper lightly but—and this is a big but—are we going to wind up with a uniform shade?

We have all seen the beautiful toning and shading effects used on manufactured furniture, especially on the maple reproductions of primitives now so popular. By shading, we mean the gradual darkening or bleeding effects. For example, we have before us a factory-finished panel of a door belonging to a reproduction of a Dutch cupboard and we notice that the edges are much darker than the center, adding a sort of antique effect. This is very easily accomplished even by amateurs when the wiping is done with a rag. We simply seek to make the change in color gradual and not abrupt.

What is known as penetrating oil stain can be mixed at home or purchased ready mixed. If prepared at home, we use four ounces of ground color pigment with a pint of carrier made up of equal parts of turpentine, benzol and boiled linseed oil. If, however, such a pigment oil stain is to be employed beneath lacquer, it is best to use only japan drier and turpentine, leaving the benzol and boiled oil out.

# ( IX )

## *Using Oil Stains*

THERE are two ways in which wood may be finished with varnish and a color other than natural. In the first case, we would apply ready-prepared color varnish, that is a varnish to which the manufacturer has added coloring matter. (Such varnishes and their application will be dealt with later.) For instance, if we had a piece of birch which we wished to have finished in mahogany, we would simply prepare the surface properly and then apply one or two coats of mahogany color varnish. The same procedure would follow for a walnut finish.

If the same piece of birch (or any other wood for that matter) was to be finished via the stain procedure, the wood would first be colored with the proper stain and then either covered with clear varnish or clear (transparent, that is) lacquer.

This latter method is by far the most difficult although by no means beyond the skill of a patient amateur. The advantage is simply this: stains enhance the beauty of grain whereas color varnishes detract from grain structure.

There are four basic types of stains. These are classified and named after the solvents (liquid dissolvers) in which the coloring matter, whatever it may be, is placed. These solvents, or carriers as we might call them, not only dissolve the solid coloring matter but also act as a vehicle by means of which the color is carried to the wood. The solvent thereupon penetrates the cells of the wood to a greater or less extent, depending upon the nature of the wood (open or close grain) and the nature of the stain. Such a procedure is usually followed by wiping the excess stain away as uniformly as possible and then permitting the remaining solvent to evaporate. This operation is followed with a thin shellac wash, and the wood is then covered with clear varnish or lacquer. Although by no means so simple, this is the basic procedure in finishing expensive furniture.

On the whole, stains are chosen for their action on the particular kind of wood we may wish to finish, their degree of penetration, their transparency and ease of application. Some, such as oil stains, are very easy to handle, others are more difficult. Hence, the word goes out that should we pick out a stain, it would be well to gain a little experience with a test panel before we set about finishing a pet piece of furniture. The test panels should be of the same kind of wood as the furniture we are going to finish.

But first let us look into this stain business in general. Four principal solvents are used and each type of stain derives its name from the solvent employed, which may be water, oil, alcohol or other synthetic solvent. Coloring matter differs also. In most cases, dry aniline dyes are dissolved in the proper solvent, whereas in the case of most oil stains, a natural coloring matter is ground in oil to which are added other carriers or solvents.

Here we are to consider oil stains alone, the following chapters to be devoted to the preparation and application of other types of stains.

As for the home preparation of oil stain, we might well decide to abstain. They are inexpensive and are now carried in cans ranging from half-pint to quart sizes. If we wished to mix our own, we would discover that the sum total of all of the ingredients involved purchased at retail prices would cost us more than the ready-to-use article, which comes in mahogany (red and brown), cherry, walnut, dark oak, light oak, dark walnut, light walnut and maple. It will be found that by juggling a can of red mahogany with a can of brown any in-between shade may be had.

Against the advantage of great ease of application as in the case of oil stain, there is the disadvantage of less transparency and consequent loss of grain effects.

Another thing that we must keep in mind in connection with all stains is the degree to which they raise (swell) the grain of a wood. If the grain is raised badly, so badly that sanding is required after the stain has dried, then there is always the possibility of cutting deeper than the stain has penetrated. This calls for restaining and perhaps a color much deeper than we planned and also a noticeable lack of uniformity in color, the spots where the sandpaper cut through showing up lighter in color.

As before stated, oil stains are made by mixing ground pigments (solid-color materials) with linseed oil and adding such solvents as turpentine, japan drier, benzine, each manufacturer having his own ideas about formula.

It is to be pointed out that such stains, or indeed stains of any kind, are not to be regarded as being suitable for the protection of wood without other materials being placed over them. All such stains leave the grain of the wood partially open, the stain becomes discolored and is very easily marked with water, etc. Stains are used to create color and tone and to emphasize grain structure for the purpose of intensifying beauty. Stains are also affected by light and none will hold their true color over a long period of years.

Aside from ease of application, oil stains also have the advantage of never raising the grain on wood, thereby eliminating the necessity of sanding after they are dry.

All oil stains may be diluted or lightened in color by the addition of turpentine. The degree to which we might wish to dilute them will have to be determined by test on panels or by the application of the stain on some part of the furniture where the test applications cannot be seen; for instance the underside of a table top. However, in diluting we should make sure to keep a record of the degree of dilution that will produce the desired shade. For instance, we take a teaspoonful of the stain from the can and add turpentine by teaspoonfuls until we get what we are after. Or it may be we will wish to add red mahogany to brown mahogany.

Oil stains may be applied with a brush or with a wadded piece of cloth. We seek only to produce a uniform film. There should be no effort to brush out this material. That would tend to produce a streaky effect. Rather, plenty of stain is put on, left for about ten minutes and then the excess is wiped away with a clean rag, leaving as uniform a color as possible.

As in the case of all other types of oil stain, however, we are apt to run into trouble with end grain; for instance the ends of table and chest top that are cut across grain. All of these stains are exceptionally fluid compared to paint, enamel or varnish, and all end grain acts like a sponge sucking up enormous quantities of stain and turning very dark as compared with the rest of the surface.

However, this problem may be easily solved in the following manner, and this holds not only for oil stain but for other stains as well. If, for instance, we are working on a table, or chest top, we cover the open grain ends with masking tape, applying it with sufficient pressure to prevent any seepage of stain when that part of the top is covered.

After the excess stain on the top has been wiped away, then the masking tape is removed and we treat the end grain with a highly diluted stain. Here we remember that if the treated end grain is too light we can always make it darker by the application of more stain. If it is too dark, well, that makes matters pretty difficult although we can apply sandpaper aggressively to try to reduce color.

The experts agree that oil stain should be permitted to dry for several days before any attempt is made to go on with the finishing of the surface.

Nor should we proceed immediately to varnish or lacquer directly over the oil stain. In the case of varnish, some of the color in the stain will be lifted up into the varnish with a loss of clearness in tone. Lacquer directly applied may have the same effect.

To prevent this, we use what the experts call a shellac wash, which is nothing more or less than a very thin coat of highly diluted shellac; one part white or clear shellac from the can mixed with seven parts of shellac thinner or alcohol. This, too, should be allowed to set up hard for several days. Our experts agree that shellac is not necessarily ready to be covered with other materials merely because it feels dry to the finger tips.

# ( X )

## *Finish after Staining*

ALL stains should be permitted to dry for forty-eight hours after they are applied. Once they are dry, however, it does not mean that we can proceed to cover them with varnish or lacquer without any other kind of preparation. Good finishing is not done that way. Procedure from this point on will depend a great deal upon the nature of the wood, the nature of the covering material selected and the nature of the stain.

Some stains exhibit what the trade calls a bleeding effect. For instance, if we placed clear lacquer directly over a spirit stain, the powerful solvents in the lacquer would redissolve some of the dye in the spirit stain and lift it up into the lacquer, producing a very muddy or cloudy effect. The same thing can happen with certain varnishes and stains. Hence, we must seal the stain off from the top finishing material in some manner.

But here we are talking only about close-grained woods. In the case of very open- or coarse-grained woods where we wish a smooth and not a natural finish, we must apply a filler colored with the same stain we used on the raw wood.

In the furniture trade there are two methods of finishing, one called "short," which is used on the cheaper grades of furniture and one called "long," which is used on the more expensive furniture. Let it be said here and now that it is doubtful that we will ever become skilled enough to apply the long method. If the short method is used and our work is done carefully there is no reason why we cannot produce fine finish, good enough for any home.

In the use of the long method, as many as three or four experts may be used in a factory to produce one operation in which they specialize. As an example, it is doubtful that the one who applies the original coat of stain will be doing the rubbing on the final coat of varnish.

The short system as far as the manufacturer of furniture is concerned usually involves semiporous or nonporous wood. The finishing operation follows:

1. Wiping stain
2. Sealer (shellac)
3. Sanding
4. Finishing coat

On the other hand, the long system involves:

1. Bleaching
2. Sanding
3. Staining
4. Wash coat
5. Sanding
6. Filling
7. Toning
8. Glazing sealer
9. Sanding
10. Glazing or high-lighting
11. Sealing
12. Sanding
13. Uniforming
14. First top coat
15. Sanding
16. Second top coat
17. Waxing

Not many amateurs, no matter how ambitious, will wish to master the seventeen operations involved in the so-called long system nor will some of these special operations be covered in this treatise.

Of course, if coarse-grained wood is being treated, the four operations in the so-called short system will have to be extended to six. After the stain is applied and is permitted to dry, a filler colored with the same stain (this will be covered in another chapter) will have to be applied over the stain and this in turn will have to be sanded.

It will be understood, of course, that stained surfaces, no matter what stain we employ, are not to be left merely stained. They will have little beauty and little durability. While it is true that oil stains having linseed oil in them will dry with a certain gloss, it will not be an attractive gloss or a gloss that will be long lasting. Nor will it be a gloss that we can improve to any great extent although we may rub the surface up a bit with wax. The solvents in most waxes will tend to pick up the coloring matter in the stain and effect unequal distribution. Stains were never intended for such use. They are strictly mediums for producing colors to be used underneath transparent surfaces that can resist wear, increase beauty, etc.

Such transparent materials may take the form of clear lacquer or varnish or white or orange shellac or one of the ultramodern plastic materials. Of course, varnish and lacquer can be had in either clear (transparent, that is) or colored. When varnish is colored it may be called varnish stain or just colored varnish, which comes in shades of walnut, mahogany, etc. However, we would not wish to use either colored varnish or lacquer over a stained surface. The use of stain would be senseless under such conditions. Varnish stain or colored varnish is used over a clean surface that has been sanded and filled or sanded and sealed with a light coat of shellac. This offers a quick way of finishing by staining and varnishing in one operation, but like most things that are done quickly, it does not offer the beauty of finish that we may have by exercising a little care and taking a little more time. The practice of staining first and then covering with either clear varnish or lacquer will permit the grain to show through, and that is the chief source of beauty.

If a colored filler is used over a stain on a coarse-grained wood, then it will be necessary to sand this after it has dried and also to cover it with a sealer such as thinned shellac if varnish is to be used or a special sealer for lacquer if lacquer is to be used.

Many amateur refinishers inquire as to the use of shellac for a finishing coat. It can indeed be used and makes a beautiful surface if applied well and rubbed gently. However, shellac is far from a durable finish. It is easily scratched and easily stained with water, etc. It is certainly not recommended for table, chest or stand tops.

There are several types of clear varnishes that may be applied. There is ordinary oil-base varnish that dries rather slowly, plastic varnishes that set up very quickly and then there is what is known as rubbing varnish which is supposed to be treated with pumice or rottenstone after it dries. Of course, ordinary varnish can also be hand rubbed with the above materials if we wish although it will probably cut a little faster and we will have to be a bit more careful near the edges. (See Chapter XII, dealing with hand rubbing.)

No matter what type of varnish is used, it is put on with a varnish brush but not before the sealing coat, no matter what it may be, is carefully treated with fine steel wool and the dust from such treatment carefully wiped away with a clean cloth dampened either with water or turpentine.

If you are applying an ordinary varnish which dries rather slowly and thereby greatly increases the dust problem, it is best to use two thin applications rather than one thick one. Varnish applied from the can in one rather thick coat naturally takes longer to dry than does varnish that has been thinned with the thinner recommended by the manufacturer on the can label.

The above holds true for ordinary glossy varnish, dull varnish, rubbing varnish, lacquer or plastic varnishes. However, in any case, steel wool is applied after the first coat has set up. Such an application of steel wool over the second coat will depend upon what sort of finish you wish. If you find that the glossy varnish you employed is far too shiny to suit your taste remember that this gloss can very easily be cut down to any degree by the use of fine steel wool, after which furniture wax may be applied and rubbed up to a very desirable soft gloss. Indeed this same procedure may be used in any of the finishing materials mentioned, including lacquer and plastic varnish. It may be that the dull varnish which is supposed to simulate a hand-rubbed effect will be too dull. If this is so, the treatment will be fine steel wool and the subsequent application of wax will bring up a fine luster. The application of steel wool is made to give the finished surface "tooth" to hold the wax.

If a very high polish is desired (a little old-fashioned these days!) we will find the directions for producing such surfaces in Chapter XII, dealing with hand rubbing.

Perhaps this might be a good spot to insert a few words about oil finish. This finish is produced with three elements, linseed oil, turpentine and enough "elbow grease" to paint a house. To produce this finish, one simply applies oil and rubs time and time again. A good job will require several weeks' time. No finish requires a longer time or produces *less* satisfactory results.

For one thing, the oil greatly darkens any wood and the oil grows continuously darker over the years. A beautiful piece of fine cherry wood can instantly be changed to a mud color by an application of oil and turpentine. And, although weeks of hard work are required to produce such a finish, it is by no means durable. It is very easily stained and requires a rubbing up with fresh oil every year or so.

Hence, if you wish to learn how to produce this finish you will have to seek your information elsewhere. The writer once spoiled a beautiful antique table in cherry by the use of this finish and he has no desire to induce other people to duplicate such a tragedy.

# ( XI )

# *Using Wood Fillers*

WOODS with open grain are often treated with a substance known as wood filler, which amounts to a paste used with different colors, different ingredients and different consistencies, depending upon the conditions to be met. When wood fillers set up, they should be hard but still able to take finishing material.

Colored filler is able to serve in two ways: it fills grain and substitutes for a stain. Indeed its function as a stain needs close study by those who seek a certain shade or tone for their work. Where colorless filler is employed, the worker may exercise complete control over ultimate color by the choice of the correct oil stain, but where one of the standard ready-mix colored fillers is used, little control may be exercised over ultimate tone and color. Again the writer recommends to the beginner the advisability of using a few test piece before he smears up a job with something that he will not like.

There are three principal types of wood fillers. One is transparent and is used on the better grades of wood where the cell openings or grain channels are so small as to be invisible to the eye. Use is indicated on such wood only when the worker seeks the finest finish, requiring a high buff. For an ordinary satin finish, there is little need for such preparation. Really such so-called fillers amount to little more than a sizing. The experts, when seeking flawless results, use such filler material on even the better grades of mahogany, walnut, etc.

In the earlier days, filling such wood was often accomplished by repeated applications of a drying oil such as linseed. Each application was followed by a long period of waiting for oxidation and then rubbing. The application of linseed oil always darkens any wood and many applications darken it still more. This procedure of wood filling is no longer recommended.

If a reader of this book desires to take his chances in producing the ultimate in a highly buffed surface, he may bring about a good foundation for his labors by applying clear shellac, highly cut, as a wood filler on the hard woods with finer grain. At least a fifty-fifty mixture of the shellac thinner should be used with shellac as it comes from the can. Two coats with very light sanding between, using No. 3/0 paper, are advised. About six to eight hours should be allowed between coats to avoid a gummy effect in the in-between sanding operations. It will be understood, of course, in the case of using oil stain, that the stain must be applied before the shellac.

The liquid fillers (the shellac is in the so-called transparent class) are not used a great deal in refinishing furniture except on woods like chestnut where grain is enormously large. These fillers are excellent for such use and also as fillers for new, open-grain woodwork in homes. Such fillers are painted on in the manner of varnish and they do not have to be rubbed off as in the case of the paste fillers which will be treated next.

Paste fillers contain drying oils and a material like silex. A gallon of such stuff will cover about 250 square feet. It can be purchased ready mixed. It is recommended that all such fillers be followed by the use of No. 2/0 sandpaper after they have set up. If a wood such as pine is to be varnished, the use of this filler is indicated.

As before stated, most woods, and this goes even for some of the less desirable grades of mahogany, require the use of a paste filler. The solid material used in such fillers may be one of a number of things but the better wood fillers sold in cans usually have a form of silica called silex as the solid material. This is carried in a thick mass and may include such other materials as boiled linseed oil, japan drier, turpentine, naphtha, benzene, and coloring matter. As supplied by the trade, such fillers are usually far too thick for use and must be thinned by the addition of turpentine or benzene.

These paste fillers are usually supplied in white or the following colors: ebony, red, brown, light and dark mahogany, natural or transparent, antique, golden oak, walnut and dark oak. Painters' pigments ground in oil are used as coloring material in paste fillers.

In a very large measure, the colors in which paste wood fillers are supplied indicate the woods upon which they are to be used; the brown mahogany on wood of that nature and color, the red mahogany for red mahogany, etc. White filler is intended for general use where color varnish or fine enamel jobs are to be used on open-grain woods.

Beginners are very apt to underestimate the degree of skill required in the successful application of paste wood fillers. For one thing, if any large amount of work is to be done with wood fillers, then it might be advisable to purchase a special brush intended for this use solely. A stiff, coarse brush is best so that the thinned paste will be pushed down into the cell and grain openings.

Before a paste filler is applied, the wood flour from all previous sanding must be removed from the grain where it is impacted. Otherwise plugged grain will greatly interfere with the successful use of the filler. An ordinary small scrubbing brush may be used to remove wood flour, the workman pressing down rather hard and always moving parallel with the grain. The final residue of dislodged wood flour is removed with a clean, slightly damp cloth.

There are many ways of using paste fillers, some of them involving surfaces that have already been colored by water or oil stains. Such use requires a judgment and skill that must come with experience. The beginner is advised to confine his use of such fillers to the treatment of deeply grained surfaces where he either wishes to apply a smooth coat of enamel or color varnish or to preserve as far as possible the natural color of a coarse-grained wood such as mahogany or walnut by the use of a clear varnish. One should proceed very cautiously, however, where either the clear or colored lacquers are to be employed over surfaces that have been treated with wood fillers. The powerful solvents in some such materials may lift up some of the oils in the filler and give an unwanted muddy effect. It is difficult in this treatment to provide an all-inclusive answer to such a problem. Any of the oil varnishes are safe to use but the expert at the paint store should be consulted in connection with lacquer because formulas of materials vary. Only a warning can be issued here.

In determining the degree of thinning before a paste filler is applied, the worker should be guided by the directions on the can. Error in making the mixture too thin by the addition of too much turpentine is to be preferred over producing too thick a mixture that will not flow down into the wood grain. The slight damage coming from too thin a mixture may always be repaired by a second coat of the same consistency. It is an invariable rule that relatively thin mixtures should be placed on wood with small grain and thicker applications made on wood with coarser grain. In no case should the consistency be thinner than that of undiluted varnish. If the mixture drops too quickly from the brush, it is probably too thin. On the other hand, if it shows no inclination to drop from the brush at all, or very slowly, it is probably too thick.

In the application of wood filler of this type the workman seeks to overcome his habits of economy by failing to brush out the mixture. One always sees to it that paste fillers are put on in healthy excess. Also the mixture is constantly stirred to keep the solid material in suspension.

While some of the old-timers insist that paste fillers should be applied in the manner of varnishes, that is moving the brush with the grain, others insist that the paste should be brushed across the grain. With no claim to being an expert, the writer takes a more logical position. To ensure the filler reaching the very bottom of the grain, the first brushing should be with the grain. This is followed by a second brushing across the grain, which should fill it.

The length of time a paste filler is allowed to set up before the excess is removed from the surface of the wood is important. Otherwise the removal of the excess may take out some of the impacted material and leave an indifferent surface. Here it is advisable to read carefully the directions on the can.

In any event, the excess of paste filler is removed by brushing *across* the grain with a heavy piece of clean burlap. This subjects the wood filler to a crosswise, shearing action which makes its surface flush with the main surface of the wood upon which it is used. It will be seen that even a small amount of lengthwise rubbing will be bound to dislodge some of the filler in the grain.

As a general rule, although the direction on cans in which wood fillers come may advise differently, one does not attempt to remove excess filler until the slight gloss has disappeared and the material no longer appears wet.

In the event of using such a filler on carved surfaces, extra care will have to be exercised in removal. In such cases it might be possible to work with a small piece of burlap or with a discarded toothbrush for the crevices.

All surfaces are somewhat rough after the filler has dried. It is therefore necessary to go over them lightly first with No. 1/o sandpaper and then with No. 3/o. This is used on a soft undersurface to prevent cutting through the film of filler. The little sanding tools in which abrasive cloth is placed over a base of sponge rubber are excellent for this purpose. A thick pad of cloth glued to a block of wood will also serve nicely and such a soft sanding block is convenient to have about the workshop.

As a final operation on such a surface, a cloth soaked in untreated petrol, benzene or naphtha is used to carry away the filler dust left by the sandpapering.

In the case of borderline woods with grain that is not especially coarse or fine, the use of a paste filler might be depended upon whether or not a water stain was used. Water stains raise the grain of the wood a great deal and therefore may place a piece of wood in need of filling.

The following table may help the beginner to decide whether or not he will need to use a filler and what type it should be for the finishing job at hand:

| Use Shellac or Other Liquid Filler | Paste Filler Only with Water Stain—Otherwise Shellac or Liquid Filler | Paste Filler of Proper Color |
|---|---|---|
| Basswood | Beech | Ash |
| Cedar | Birch | Beech |
| Cypress | Boxwood | Elm |
| Ebony | Cherry | Chestnut |
| Fir | Cottonwood | Mahogany |
| Hemlock | Gumwood | Locust |
| Holly | Maple, hard and | Oak |
| Magnolia | soft | Rosewood |
| Spruce | Sycamore | Walnut (all kinds) |
| Pine, both yellow and white | Redwood | Hickory |
| Poplar or whitewood | | Satinwood |
| Deal | | |

As a mixing guide for thinning wood fillers the worker may use the following table supplied by one of the manufacturers of such materials:

| LIGHT MIX | | MEDIUM MIX | | HEAVY MIX | |
|---|---|---|---|---|---|
| Paste | Thinner | Paste | Thinner | Paste | Thinner |
| 5 lbs. | 2½ pts. | 5 lbs. | 3 lbs. 5. oz. | 5 lbs. | 5 pts. |
| 1 qt. | 1 qt. | 1 qt. | 2 pts. 10 oz. | 1 qt. | 2 qts. |
| 1 pt. | 1 pt. | 1 pt. | 1 pt. 5 oz. | 1 pt. | 2 pts. |
| 1 lb. | ½ pt. | 1 lb. | 10½ oz. | 1 lb. | 1 pt. |
| ½ lb. | 4 oz. | ½ lb. | 5¼ oz. | ½ lb. | ½ pt. |

If stirring is not constantly resorted to, the filler applied to the last of a large surface may be much thicker or thinner than that applied first, depending upon how deeply the workman had gone into the bottom of the can.

It will be noticed that immediately after the filler has been applied it has a slight gloss to it. As this is replaced by a dullness, the filler is ready to remove. It is usually recommended that fillers be left in place no longer than a few minutes. Thus the worker may find himself towing off (wiping off) at one end of the job (the first) while the last filler applied to the piece is not yet ready. One watches for the dullness to appear and goes to work immediately.

This so-called towing-off is done with a piece of burlap, tow or any other suitable material of this nature. Inasmuch as a thin film of filler left after the towing or wiping will soon set up hard, the worker should not plan on returning to a spot. Rather he should finish his work as he moves along, at all times wiping across the grain to produce a shearing action which will leave the filler deposited in the grain. Frequent changes of wiping material may be necessary for larger surfaces.

If the worker should be caught off guard and find himself up against a patch of filler that has set up too hard, then he should moisten this with an application of naphtha followed by a second application of filler. This is then removed in the approved manner after becoming dull in appearance.

In the case of corners or lightly carved surfaces, a pointed matchstick should be used to remove all excess material before it has a chance to set up.

After the towing-off process, a final wiping is done with a soft rag. This should follow the towing-off immediately and before the residue of filler has had a chance to set up. It might help to moisten the soft rag with naphtha as a final wipe. All of this wiping may be done with and across the grain for this really amounts to a cleaning-up operation.

A quick-drying filler in which naphtha has been used as a thinning agent should set up in about eight hours. A slow-drying filler, using gum turpentine, may require as many as thirty-six hours for setting up.

After setting up, the filler is sealed with a very thin coat of shellac or lacquer sealer. It is to be pointed out here that many fillers made during the past few years are available for overcoats of both lacquer and enamel. After this sealer coat has dried, it is sanded lightly with No. 3/0 sandpaper. After the dust has been brushed away, an undiluted coat of the final finish, whether lacquer or varnish, should be applied. This is a foundation coat and should therefore be rubbed with waterproof sandpaper of a very fine grade. Then the final coat of varnish or lacquer, as the case may be, is applied.

As before stated, ready-mixed wood fillers may now be purchased in all the common colors as well as natural and white. It is quite possible that every worker will be able to purchase just the right color for the job at hand. If he cannot do this, it is easy to change the color of natural or white wood filler with the addition of suitable oils and pigments. It may be that a mahogany filler already at hand is to be made darker. In any event, procedure is as follows:

Ordinary oil colors are first mixed in turpentine, the worker bearing in mind that a small amount of such color goes a long way and that it is better by far to err on the side of too little than too much. The thinned oil colors are added to the wood filler after it has been thinned and the worker stirs patiently until he obtains perfect uniformity.

Although considered a short cut, some workers mix ordinary oil stains with wood fillers before the latter are applied. This may save the trouble of placing a coat of stain on the work before the wood filler is put on.

In the case of raised grain, filler has not been given sufficient drying time. Pinholes may be caused by the filler being too thick, and gray pores result from lack of sufficient drying time and from the filler being too light in color. Of course, streaky or cloudy effects are due to poor wiping.

No paste filler is needed for woods such as basswood, cedar, cypress, fir, hemlock, pine, poplar, spruce or willow. A thin filler is usually advisable for alder, beech, birch, boxwood, cherry, ironwood, maple or sycamore. Medium fillers may be applied to butternut, mahogany (of certain grades), rosewood and walnut. Thick fillers are required by ash, chestnut, locust, oak, teak and the softer mahoganies with large grain.

In case the worker does not have data on the proper color mixtures for coloring fillers with ground oils, the following will help:

*Black*—Add drop black to natural filler. Suitable for black-wood or dark mahogany.

*White*—Color natural base with zinc oxide. Used for limed oak and similar effects on chestnut and ash.

*Light Brown*—Tint with Vandyke brown to required shade. Can be used on any light-brown wood.

*Dark Brown*—Vandyke brown with a touch of drop black. For walnut, mahogany, etc. Suitable for any medium to dark-colored wood.

*Walnut*—Half and half Vandyke brown and burnt umber.

*Light Red*—Use any red color (Indian red) in oil or japan, toning darker or lighter with drop black or zinc white.

*Dark Red*—Equal parts of burnt umber and rose pink. Add drop black for darker shade. Used for Sheraton mahogany or any other red finish where dark pores are desirable.

*Amber*—Tint natural base with yellow or orange oil colors. Suitable for ambered walnut, harvest-wheat mahogany and other bleached finishes.

# ( XII )

# *Hand Rubbing Is Easy*

THE hand rubbing and polishing of varnished surfaces is practiced not only in finishing the top or ultimate surface but also between coats of varnish in an effort to build up a smooth top surface. If a first coat of varnish is permitted to set up with dust specks or roughness from other causes we cannot expect that another coat will cure the condition. Again we repeat that any coat of paint, varnish or enamel cannot produce smoothness that is not in some degree present in the surface beneath. Hence in multicoat finishes, experts always work up each succeeding coat by hand rubbing before another coat is applied.

Several mediums exist for such hand rubbing. First we have the ultrafine grit waterproof papers in garnet, aluminum oxide, etc. These are always used with water as a lubricant, the water serving to slow the cutting action and bring it under better control. Such papers are, however, pretty fast cutting for amateur use although they are widely employed for between-coat preparation in furniture factories.

Often the final coat of finishing lacquer as applied in furniture factories is rubbed with No. 360 paper lubricated with a thinner such as Exolvent mixed fifty-fifty with paraffin oil. This is a rough-over hand rubbing which is immediately followed by rubbing with a mixture of pumice powder and rottenstone applied with a felt pad and paraffin oil alone. In all rubbing operations, much will depend upon the wishes of the worker and what sort of a surface pleases him.

Pumice powder or rottenstone powder is much safer in the hands of amateurs for the simple reason that they cut more slowly. Pumice may be used alone or it may be followed by the use of rottenstone. It all depends upon the sort of polish you wish

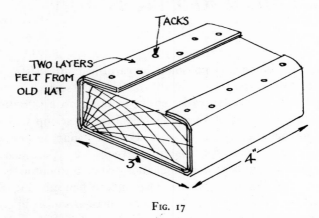

FIG. 17

Hand-rubbing device for use with pumice or rottenstone. It is made by tacking several layers of an old felt hat to a block of wood.

to have. Pumice is used first because it is slightly coarser than rottenstone. Both of these materials may be purchased by the pound at any good hardware or paint store. They are inexpensive and one-half pound of each will do a great deal of rubbing.

Pumice and rottenstone are also used with lubricants, which may be water, various oil combinations or ordinary crude oil. The oils still further reduce the cutting action and are therefore recommended over water for amateur use.

Pumice and rottenstone rubbing is never done with the bare hands. To start with, it would be pretty rough on the hands and then there is the matter of equalized pressure. Rather the rubbing is always done with felt. This felt may come from an old felt hat (see Fig. 17), or it may come in the form of a solid felt slab

$\frac{1}{4}$ to $\frac{1}{2}$ inch thick and measuring about 3 x 5 inches. Such felt slabs may be purchased by the ounce in large paint-supply houses.

If we propose using crude oil as a lubricant for our pumice, it will be good to wet the rubbing surface of such a felt with the oil before we start a job.

We start rubbing by dusting some of the dry pumice on that part of a surface upon which work is begun. Then crude oil is poured on and the rubbing pad is used to mix the pumice and the oil into a thin paste with the consistency of cream. If there is too much or too little of one ingredient or the other, one or the other is added to balance things.

In rubbing we apply only moderate pressure until we get used to this business and the refinishing of a single piece of furniture is not enough to make us experts, however puffed up we may feel about the final result.

It is advisable in rubbing to go with the grain. Experts do not always do this especially with rottenstone but it is the safest procedure.

It is also necessary to achieve as much uniformity as possible by working over the entire surface with an equal amount of rubbing.

The greatest danger lies in working near the edges of a table or chest top or any edge for that matter. When working on an edge, there will be a tendency to increase the pressure between the edge and the rubbing felt thereby increasing cutting action. Unless we are very careful, all varnish will be removed from such edges and we may easily cut down into the wood itself, thereby destroying all color. When such a condition develops, we will be in real trouble and we will be faced with the prospect of a complete refinishing job.

If the felt used for rubbing flat surfaces is used on round surfaces such as legs, we will also be faced with the danger of cutting through the finish because of the increase of pressure between the felt and the small segment of surface being worked upon. To prevent this we should use a small piece of an old felt hat and wrap it around the leg, working the felt up and down with the grain.

After all rubbing has been completed, we should wash the surface with turpentine, followed by mild soap and warm water with a good rinsing with clean warm water.

After the surface is dry, we apply a good grade of furniture wax and rub it up briskly until the proper polish is achieved.

If we wish a superpolish or a very high gloss surface (not in favor these days) the use of rottenstone is continued until such a high gloss is achieved. In such a case, very little rottenstone is employed with plenty of oil. Rubbing will have to be patiently continued far beyond the point where ordinary rubbing is completed. This high polish is often referred to as French polish. It has long since gone out of date.

# ( XIII )

## How to Use a Spray Gun

ALTHOUGH most of the marvelous new enamels or enamel-like colorings can be applied just as smoothly by brush as by means of the spray, it must be confessed that the spray gun is ideal for a material like lacquer. Barring fillers, all other materials can be sprayed—paint, shellac, varnish, stains, etc.—providing they are thinned sufficiently. Directions for thinning are usually included on container labels.

Spraying equipment is supplied in a wide range both of price and size. There is also the spraying outfit supplied with many home vacuum cleaners, a very useful article indeed if we wish to employ it for jobs within its scope. One would not, however, set out to paint a house with it. One would not hesitate, however, to use such modest equipment in applying highly diluted lacquer or ordinary stain.

Other spray equipment with motor may run in price all the way from $25 to over $300 for professional, heavy-duty machinery. It is also to be recalled that many large hardware stores and some paint shops rent out such equipment for a small hourly fee.

For ordinary jobs such as applying a finish like Kem-Glo to furniture, we need not worry about spraying equipment. The brush will do the job almost as quickly or even more quickly if we seek two color effects or striping. Where walls are to be finished, then there might be some advantage in spraying to gain time although there will be no advantage in final appearance, something that could not be said a few years ago with the old-fashioned paints in use at that time.

We will not be interested here in going into detail concerning types of guns and equipment. Rather our interest will lie in

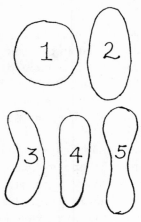

FIG. 18

Spray gun patterns possible with adjustable nozzles. (1) Round spray, (2) fan spray, (3) kidney pattern, (4) heavy end pattern, (5) split pattern.

adjusting spray guns so as to obtain the proper pattern of spray and in the manipulation of such equipment to ensure an even distribution.

Figure 18 shows the several types of spray patterns along with the ideal adjustment, which will in some measure depend upon the nozzle design of the spray gun employed. It is most important that we achieve a good spray pattern before work is begun. Old newspapers held to a wall with scotch tape will permit experimentations with nozzle adjustment until we have a good pattern.

Figure 19 will show how it is that so many people have poor results in spraying. In all cases, the spray gun nozzle should be held about six to eight inches from the surface being sprayed. Any serious variation in this distance will make for poor, uneven

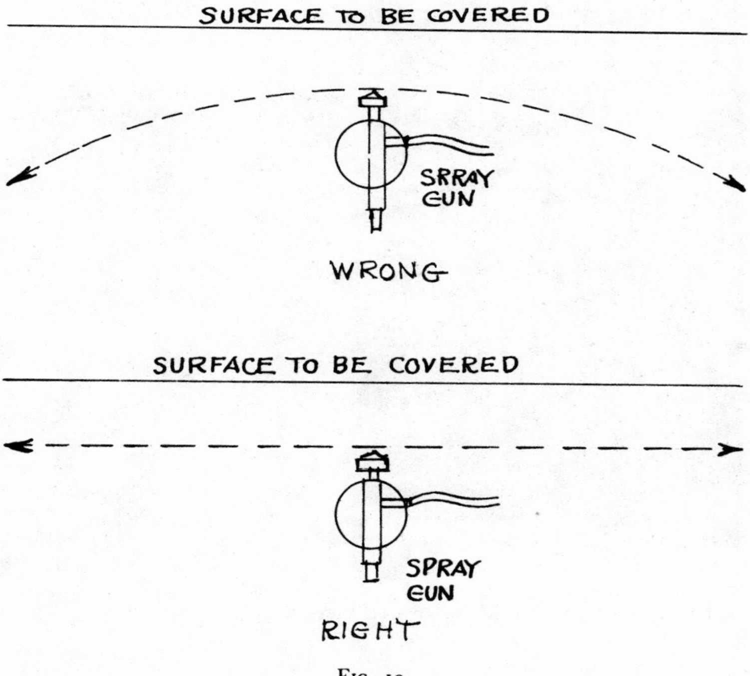

FIG. 19

Right (lower) and wrong (upper) spray gun sweep.

distribution of the covering material. As will be noted, many beginners make the mistake of swinging the spray gun in an arc. In such cases, the spray will thin out considerably at each end of the swing for the reason that the gun nozzle will be farther away from its target. All sprays fan out as they leave the nozzle of the gun. This sort of application will also cause the sprayed material to build up heavily at the point where it comes closest to the surface being sprayed.

Naturally, the first rule in the successful use of a spray gun is

FIG. 20

Vacuum-cleaner-type spray gun which may be used with modern enamels, lacquer, etc.

to keep it moving at a uniform speed. Stopping even momentarily will cause the finishing material to pile up too thickly. We must also learn to "feather off" at the end of each stroke or swing and to overlap each stroke about one half.

It is recommended that we practice with a spray gun on newspapers for at least one hour before we make an attempt to do serious work. Two or three hours' practice with a thinned-down can of old enamel would be much better if the old enamel has not reached the point where it has developed a skin over its top surface. Spray gun nozzles have very small openings that are easily clogged and material sprayed must be clean.

FIG. 21

Spraying from a pressure-type can with enamels. Such ready-to-spray enamels come in 12 colors.

After each job, the nozzle of the spray gun and the container are thoroughly washed with either turpentine, Exolvent or untreated gasoline. It will be evident that in spraying a quick-setting material like lacquer, we cannot begin and then set the gun down for an hour or so without using it.

If we are spraying a surface where there is danger of overspray striking another surface, we simply use old newspapers or a cardboard shield to protect such surfaces.

If we are spraying lacquer or certain other materials having solvents that may produce toxic effects, we are warned to have plenty of ventilation. If we can do our work in a garage with the doors open, so much the better.

The degree of thinning for lacquer, paint, etc., will in some measure depend upon the material and the work. Lacquer is usually used about fifty-fifty; that is, for every cupful of lacquer we use a cupful of the thinner recommended by the manufacturer of the lacquer. Naturally such coats of lacquer are thin and perhaps several applications will be needed.

Shellac should be thinned even more, but here again several coats may be needed except in cases where shellac is used as a sealer where a 1-5 mixture may be employed.

The various synthetic enamels should be thinned down, using only the thinner made by the manufacturer of the particular material we are using and to the extent recommended by the manufacturer. Such material is first applied in a very thin sprayed coat. After this becomes tacky, we adjust the nozzle of the gun for the application of a full wet coat which is immediately applied.

It should be mentioned here that the spray gun is ideal in applying stencils to walls or furniture.

# ( XIV )

# Refinishing Old Pine and Maple

MANY collectors of antiques wish to refinish old pine and maple in such a manner as to preserve as far as possible the patina of such woods. Wood undergoes a slow chemical change over the years, becoming darker and on the whole more beautiful especially from the standpoint of indicating age. This is especially true of pine. Pine, after a hundred years or more, reaches a warm, nut-brown color much worth keeping. Such a color enhances the value of an antique from the viewpoint of a collector who knows what he is about. The following procedure will preserve this patina.

Even though an old pine piece will reach us in a painted condition, upon the removal of the paint it will be found that the wood is of a color that will delight the heart of a connoisseur. However, the removal of the paint may be laborious because of the extreme hardness of the first coat which may underlie several others. It is not only necessary to use plenty of modern varnish remover in such cases but the scraper as well. Here, however, we must be extremely careful to prevent the sharp edges of such scrapers from digging into the soft pine to a point below the patina. While it is true that the color of all old wood is changed all the way through, it is also true that the maximum color change takes place on the surface. Hence, we try to preserve this surface as far as possible.

We must, however, remove the discoloration left by the paint and the last vestige of the paint itself, which will require patience.

After the last of the paint has been removed, we sand the surface rather gently with No. 3/0 sandpaper, trying to remove only enough wood to leave the true patina. After the sandpaper is used, we then apply fine steel wool and rub it briskly, which in itself produces a certain beautiful bloom on the old wood. All traces of dust are removed with a clean rag moistened with turpentine.

The finish is very simple and has been used for many years by the writer. It never fails to produce a fine effect that lasts for a long time although it is not recommended for table tops. On the other hand, we will find very few table tops made of pine.

The finishing material is made of a fifty-fifty mixture of high-grade shellac, $\frac{1}{2}$ brown and $\frac{1}{2}$ white. When put on, it will create a honey tone that fits in handsomely with the natural color of the old pine.

If we wish we can apply three or four coats, sanding lightly between each, or we may use only two coats with slight thinning and light sanding between the first and second.

After the shellac has set up for twenty-four hours, we go over it with fine steel wool to create "tooth" for a light-colored furniture wax that is applied last and rubbed up. The result will be "a skin you will love to touch" and the color will be entirely appropriate.

If ordinary amber-colored varnish is applied to such a surface, you may live to regret it. It will tend to darken the wood color and will grow darker with age much faster than will the shellac mixture. Water-white varnish may also be employed but with no advantage over the shellac.

The same shellac mixture may be applied over old maple if we so wish but here it might be more advisable to use a water-white varnish or, if we used shellac, the white shellac alone. However, shellac should never be applied to a table top, because it lacks durability.

Water-white or very clear lacquer is much better for table tops than varnish because it is proof against alcohol and other things which will stain or partially dissolve other varnish-type finishes. In case we have had trouble with lacquer and wish to avoid any further experience with it, we may turn to one of the several alcohol-proof varnishes on the market.

Above all we are warned against applying a plain linseed oil finish to either one of these woods. The result will be horrible to behold. The color will be deepened to mud and all of the true patina will be utterly lost with no known method of bringing it back. Oil penetrates to such a depth that removal would call for scraping beyond the depth of the patina, and the use of solvents would only dissolve the oil and carry it far deeper. What about bleach? we may ask. Well, frankly, the writer has never seen an oiled surface so treated but he hates to think about it.

# ( XV )

# Refinishing Antiques in Walnut and Mahogany

IF YOU have never before had experience in stripping and refinishing mahogany, walnut or rosewood antiques and you have an eighteenth-century highboy or an eighteenth-century slant desk upon which you would like to work, take a tip. It is not good to start operations on such expensive things. A mid-Victorian chair or an early Victorian sofa, yes; but until you gather in some experience in refinishing in general, it is best to let the good items stand until you feel that you can do a job worthy of them.

Really there is little difference between the refinishing of an antique and any other article save that we do not wish to have our antique chair or whatever it may be appear as though it has just come out of a furniture shop. In short, we will wish as far as possible to make our finish antique or old in appearance. This can be very easily done and "here's how."

As an example, let us assume that we are refinishing a mid- or early-Victorian chest of drawers, one of those with the exquisite plume-type crotch mahogany veneer on all of the drawer fronts.

Removing the varnish from such furniture is no more difficult than removing it from any other object. Nothing but the modern removers, either paste or fluid, should be used. Here we try to avoid the use of anything like a hook-type scraper for fear of digging into the thin veneer on the drawer fronts. This can produce ugly wounds and ugly wounds will leave ugly scars no matter how diligently we strive to patch them up and conceal them.

We will wish especially to remove every last speck of old varnish from the veneer on the drawer fronts by the use of the solvent alone if at all possible, even though it takes a quart of the preparation. Heavy burlap for wiping will be more effective than soft cloths.

After all of the varnish is removed, we wash the surface with turpentine and then go over it gently with No. 3/0 or No. 4/0 garnet or sandpaper to open up the pores of the mahogany veneer. Up to this point we will probably be disappointed, but let us not despair. The big thrill is yet to come. Up to this point the surface will appear dull and without the color we seek. After the application of the sandpaper, we apply the usual treatment of fine steel wool, which is followed by another turpentine or Exolvent wash to remove the fine wood dust.

After this we make a mixture of one part linseed oil and three parts of turpentine and apply it to the surface of the mahogany veneer with a clean rag. Just a thin film will do, but what a change will be wrought by it! There is no greater thrill in refinishing than that observed by the magic change brought about in veneer by such an application. Tremendous contrast and luster are produced immediately. The same will also hold in the case of rosewood.

The excess oil-turpentine mixture is wiped off within a half hour with a clean rag, and the surface is rubbed up a bit with another clean soft rag. After another forty-eight hours of drying, it is ready for an application of regular varnish. You are warned not to attempt to place lacquer over this oil base. If you must use lacquer over veneer then the veneer must be left without the oil-turpentine treatment.

To ensure uniform distribution of the varnish, the drawer

fronts should be laid horizontal while the varnish is being applied. The same holds for lacquer if that is used.

As for the type of varnish, high gloss or dull, the choice must be left to the worker. In any event, we will wish to go over it with fine steel wool, remove the dust and then wax and buff the surface with a smooth cloth.

If the remainder of the chest is plain mahogany, we will follow the same procedure save that we may wish to change the tone or shade of the mahogany with stain. If we give this plain mahogany the oil-turpentine treatment, it could turn out too red to offer real contrast to the drawer fronts. This could be changed by using a brown stain on the plain mahogany top and sides, followed by the same varnish treatment used on the drawer fronts.

Most mahogany side chairs will appear pretty anemic from a color standpoint after they have been completely stripped and sanded. The writer has refinished many of them for his own home and for the homes of friends. He invariably found that either brown or red stain had to be applied to bring out the color desired by the worker. However, some red mahogany stains on the market are so violently red when applied to open mahogany that one should try a smear on the underside of the chair being finished before the final decision is made. You are warned that sanded mahogany is a very, very thirsty wood and that once it is covered with stain the stain will sink in so deeply that removal or even reduction of tone becomes a very knotty problem quite beyond the solution of amateurs.

The use of steel wool over the varnish and the application of wax provide a beautiful soft luster finish that fits any kind of an antique, and such finishes are very easy to produce. They are also practical. An application of furniture wax will quickly restore them to the condition they were in five minutes after they were finished originally.

# ( XVI )

## Finishing Unfinished Furniture

TODAY the furniture market places are filled with various forms of unpainted furniture; bookcases, shelves, chests, etc. The wood used varies greatly but most of it is intended to be covered with modern enamels applied in the form of any color combination the purchaser wishes.

Color selection will be left to the reader, but it can be said that a two-color job is far more interesting than a one-color. For instance, a bookcase would be much better-looking if the outside was done in a pastel green and the inside of the shelves with a very light yellow. Or we might do the whole piece in green and use the yellow either on the front facing edges of the bookcase or in the form of stripes.

Striping in the professional manner may be very easily done by using masking tape applied in parallel strips as illustrated in Fig. 22. In the same figure we also see ways of protecting the edges of the furniture with masking tape until we are ready to paint them.

Of course, like all other jobs, operations are started by a good sanding with a relatively coarse (No. 1) sandpaper, which is followed by an application of No. 5/0 or No. 6/0 and a dusting off, which in turn is followed by wiping with a rag soaked in turpentine or Exolvent. This should eliminate the last speck of wood dust.

While it is quite true that the modern enamels such as Kem-Glo have terrific covering power and that in many cases a single coat will serve the purpose, it is asking a little too much of such a preparation to cover new wood with a single application. Perhaps we could flow enough such material on if the surface was horizontal, but then there would be the danger of having to flow

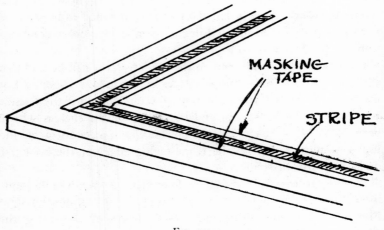

FIG. 22

How masking tape is used to paint in straight stripes on modern furniture.

it on so thickly as to run the risk of having it run off the edges.

It is better by far and on the whole winds up with a smoother job if we place a flat white coat beneath the top or finishing coat. Another twenty-four hours will be added to the time required for finishing if an undercoat is applied but it will be time well spent.

In fairness to the manufacturer whose top finish we are using, we should employ the flat coat supplied and recommended by him. It will also be necessary to brush this flat coat out smoothly and uniformly, making it as white as possible without brushing on too much.

After the top coat dries for at least twenty-four hours, it is sanded with 5/o paper, and for an extra-smooth foundation, we can follow the sanding with a brisk application of fine steel wool, after which the paint dust is wiped away with a damp cloth.

If drawers are involved in the new furniture we are refinishing, it is advisable to paint these with flat white and also to give the inside of such drawers a finishing coat, which may be the same color as the outside coat or one complimentary to it.

The instruction in Chapter VII should be followed in brushing on the enamel. Most painters brush first with the grain, then across and finally level off with the grain, applying moderate pressure uniformly. If uniform pressure is not applied, the enamel is apt to be thicker in one spot than in another.

Most beginners also try to cover too much space at a time, flowing paint on like mad until a great pool of it has been placed, after which they set about the task of distribution. Such application does not make for uniform coverage. To be sure, the enamel and enamel-like preparations do require rather copious filling of the brush and the flowing of the materials. That does not mean that we should practically dump the contents of the can on the surface and then set about desperately to brush it out.

# ( XVII )

## *Anyone Can Finish or Refinish Floors*

SO YOU wish to refinish your floor or floors? Most people look forward to such chores with dread. They had a right to in the old days, and the "old days" were just a few years back, when the marvelous new finishes were unavailable and we could not go to the hardware store and rent a power sanding machine with a dust collector attached to it. It is not yet a job that can be reduced to an evening's work, to be sure, but the really hard work has been taken from it. With friend wife as Able Assistant No. 1 the job can be done with ease in several evenings and at great savings. Several floors may be finished at a cost that would not exceed the cost of one floor done professionally.

But let us not make the sad mistake of believing that, armed with a quart of varnish remover and a scraper, we can successfully cope with a 20 x 12 foot floor with its coats of twenty-year old varnish or paint on it. For such a floor several gallons of remover would be required and we would be confined to our knees for endlessly scraping and hacking until every muscle in our body protested painfully. Better by far to rent a belt sanding machine and several fresh belts. Besides the rental of such a machine might amount to far less than would the great amount of varnish remover that would be required. And that is to say nothing about the sticky, gooey mess produced by the soft varnish. We would soon be sick of the whole thing.

That is not by any means to discount even partially the effectiveness of modern paint and varnish removers. They are quite wonderful but as beginners let us confine them to lesser jobs. Besides even after we had laboriously removed the old varnish or paint from the floor by such means we would still be faced with the job of sanding if a nice finish was to be had and sanding such a large surface by hand is not something which one may look forward to with any degree of pleasure. It is very hard work.

Of course, it is not always necessary to get "down to the wood" as the painters say. If a floor has been reasonably cared for, if it does not have large patches that have been worn through and if it is not covered with stains and nicks, all it will need is a good scrubbing and the application of a fresh coat of varnish.

For such cases we merely scrub the floor with clean soap and water to which the usual amount (for scrubbing, that is) of ammonia has been added. Any excessive amounts of ammonia might tend to soften some grades of varnish. We resolve at the beginning of such scrubbing to use plenty of clean warm water and plenty of rinsing so that as little soap deposit as possible will be left on the floor.

We also have to see to it that the cracks in the floor, if any exist, are carefully scrubbed out and given ample time to dry out. After a floor is so prepared, it is left for at least twenty-four hours before actual varnishing begins.

If such floors do have bad patches where the varnish has been broken through by furniture casters or legs, and which has become somewhat discolored at such points, we can partially if not wholly correct such conditions by working over such spots with 2/o sandpaper lubricated with turpentine. Sometimes painters also use weak bleaches on such spots, where a certain amount of dirt has actually been ground down into the wood.

If a floor is in good condition but has been long treated with wax, we must make very sure that no deposit of wax, however thin, is left. The warm water and soap should remove it.

Large cracks in old wooden floors should be filled either with the standard preparations intended for such use or with a mixture of sawdust and glue which we may prepare ourselves. Such preparations may be colored with the proper stain if such coloring is needed.

If we are working over an old finish, it will also be necessary (after the scrubbing is done and the floor is dry) to sandpaper the gloss of the old finish away with No. o sandpaper. This is followed by carefully wiping away the dust that will be left by the use of a clean cloth moistened with turpentine.

No effort should be made to save a few pennies by purchasing a cheap floor varnish. A standard varnish should be used and one that is recommended for use on floors. Such varnishes are not too brittle when dry and will take a great deal of wear.

In applying varnish we try to arrange lighting so that no spots will be left uncovered. We also make sure of our "escape" by brushing our way toward a door.

About five boards (in the case of ordinary hardwood floors) are varnished at one time all the way across the room. We then return to the starting point and take the next five boards, filling our brush rather well and brushing out firmly with long strokes.

If brand new floors are being refinished or if we have power-sanded old floors down to the wood, a quite different procedure will be necessary. If such floors are of open-grain wood such as ash or oak, it will be necessary to employ a filler. If we wish a natural color, the wood filler should be so chosen. However, if the floor is to be "walnut" or "oak" then it will be necessary to stain the wood first and apply the wood filler colored with walnut or oak, using, if possible, the same stain in the filler as was used to stain the floor.

In any event, the wood filler is thinned to about the consistency of varnish with the thinner recommended by its manufacturer. It is then brushed on the floor and permitted to set until it begins to lose its luster, at which time it is wiped away *across the grain* with rough cloths such as old burlap.

Such filler should be permitted to dry at least overnight before it is sanded with No. 2/0 paper. After the sanding, the resulting dust is wiped away with a turpentine-moistened rag or series of rags.

If a stain is used on a floor, it is usually advisable to seal the floor with a thin wash coat of shellac before the varnish is applied. In the case of varnishing a new floor or a floor that has been power-sanded down to the wood, all the preliminary preparation is followed by the application of from two to three coats of varnish with ample drying time allowed between each along with efforts to eliminate as much dust as possible.

# ( XVIII )

# *Walls, Ceilings and Woodwork*

A FEW years ago, the redecorating of a room was a pretty long and messy job and, as far as amateurs were concerned, the chances were that the results would not be too satisfactory. The materials were difficult to handle, elaborate preparations had to be made and the complete redecoration of a single room might have required as much as a week's time.

This is not so today. With two workers, a moderate-sized room might be finished in a single day. The modern finishes both for walls and woodwork set up so rapidly that two coats can be applied within a matter of four hours and the danger of brush marks and laps may be completely eliminated. Savings can be reduced to the mere cost of the materials, which is relatively low. A ten-dollar bill will be sufficient for a small room.

The following directions will be confined to Kem-Tone, Super Kem-Tone and Kem-Glo, all of them manufactured under license by a number of the larger paint manufacturers of the U.S.A. Consequently they may be purchased in any city, town or hamlet of the country.

Anyone who has used Kem-Tone understands why it is so popular. It can be easily applied on almost any kind of interior wall surface. Kem-Tone goes over wallpaper, previously painted walls, wallboard or unpainted plaster.

A gallon of Kem-Tone is adequate for the average room. A quart will do the usual ceiling area. Kem-Tone doesn't show brush marks and paint brushes can be cleaned by simply washing them with soap and water. There's no turpentine or paint thinner to buy.

Kem-Tone contains twenty-three carefully developed ingredients—pigments and colors are scientifically combined with durable oils and resins. An early criticism was that paints that thin with water were not washable. You can wash Kem-Tone oil and resin paint with even a mild solution of ordinary wall-washing compound, but you can clean a Kem-Tone painted room more easily and with much less muss by just wiping off the dirt with wallpaper cleaner.

Kem-Tone contains a thermo-tempered oil and an emulsifying agent which performs the miracle of making oil and water mix. Ordinary oil paint is thinned with turpentine or mineral spirits. On the wall the turpentine evaporates from the ordinary oil paint, from Kem-Tone the water evaporates. In both instances, the finish on the wall is a dried coating of pigments, oil, color and resins. Because Kem-Tone is made in thin paste form, it is much more economical. Through the addition of a half gallon of water, we actually get a gallon and a half of Kem-Tone ready to use on the wall.

In preparing Kem-Tone for use we must be careful not to add more than a half gallon of water to the gallon of paint. Some people prefer to use Kem-Tone in a slightly heavier consistency when it is to be applied with a roller, a painting tool specially designed for applying Kem-Tone.

If a brush is used for applying Kem-Tone, a four-inch one is recommended. We apply Kem-Tone in generous brushfuls. Keep the brushing to a minimum and level off lightly with the tip of the bristles. Ventilation will hasten and aid proper drying. In an hour or two, the draperies and furniture can be put back in place.

When time is taken out for lunch, the brush is simply immersed in the Kem-Tone or washed out with soap and water.

In most cases little or no preparation of the surface is necessary for the application of Kem-Tone. It can be painted directly over wallpaper, applying only one coat in most instances. One coat of Kem-Tone will produce a very good finish over most wallboards, but the thick spongy types will require two coats for a well-covered job. Over walls previously painted with ordinary flat wall paint we simply apply Kem-Tone in the same consistency as for wallpaper. For walls painted with a semiglossy or glossy paint, it is advisable to mix the Kem-Tone a little heavier—using three pints of water to the gallon.

We must be sure that any greasy dirt is washed off old painted walls. In the case of high gloss, it is advisable to cut the gloss by washing with a strong cleaning solution.

A touch of decorative interest may be added to a room by the use of Kem-Tone Trims, the paper borders styled and colored in perfect harmony with Kem-Tone colors. They are prepasted and simply require dipping in water before smoothing on the wall. These Kem-Tone Trims are washable, too.

After the redecoration of a room with Kem-Tone and/or Kem-Tone Vogue Deep Colors, the effect produced by the color tone and soft mat finish of these amazing paints will be delightful. Scores of lovely new colors are now available by intermixing Kem-Tone and Kem-Tone Vogue Deep Colors or by using the latter as they come in the package. Vogue Deep Colors should be applied with a roller, using two coats. Kem-Tone Vogue Deep Colors are made in shades of red, burgundy, green, yellow, brown, blue, sienna and umber.

Once you have used Kem-Tone it is always easy to redecorate. Another coat of Kem-Tone or, if desired, ordinary paint can be applied over Kem-Tone painted walls. It is also easy to remove wallpaper which has been painted with Kem-Tone.

Kem-Glo is a superb tilelike finish for walls and woodwork in kitchens, bathrooms, nurseries, playrooms, hallways and for all woodwork in every room in the house. Kem-Glo's lustrous finish matches both in appearance and washability a baked enamel finish. It requires no wall primer or enamel undercoater. This new product is easily applied with brush or roller. It comes ready to use and does not require thinning with turpentine, mineral spirits, or any other thinner.

The luster was selected for Kem-Glo to provide a maximum durability and pleasing appearance without glare. The subdued luster finish actually looks and washes like baked enamel. Of special interest to home decorators is the line of colors which were found after years of experience to be the colors most demanded for kitchens, bathrooms and woodwork. These colors, it should be noted, may be used to match or contrast with Kem-Tone colors. There are nine colors plus white, which has unusual non-yellowing properties.

In the development of Kem-Glo great emphasis was placed on the ease of application, and for the first time a finish has been developed which requires no wall primer for walls or undercoater for woodwork. In cases where two coats may be required over new wood or new plaster, Kem-Glo may be used in package consistency for both coats. Since it dries rapidly, the second coat, when necessary, may be applied within four to five hours. Therefore, with quick drying and lack of need for primer coats, a room may be completed in one day instead of the usual two or three days required for ordinary enamel finishes.

Kem-Glo is designed for the walls and woodwork of kitchens and bathrooms and for the woodwork in every room in the home. Kem-Glo, also, gives excellent results on any wood or metal surface, indoors or outdoors, where resistance to extensive scrubbings, wear and stains is required. It is ideal for kitchen and breakfast-room furniture, playroom furniture, porch and lawn furniture.

Before Kem-Glo is applied to any surface, all dirt and loose paint must be removed. To ensure the proper drying of Kem-Glo, grease or wax must be thoroughly washed off with a good household paint cleaner. High-gloss surfaces should be dulled by washing and sanding. Rough woodwork surfaces should also be sanded. All nailholes and cracks should be filled with Plastic Patch.

A gallon of Kem-Glo will cover the average kitchen walls, woodwork and cabinets. One to two quarts are required to do the woodwork in the average living room or the walls and woodwork in the average bathroom. One quart will do the woodwork in the average bedroom.

Kem-Glo should be stirred thoroughly, from the bottom of the can, with an upward motion, before the brush is dipped into it. Apply Kem-Glo in generous brushfuls, spreading evenly but not too thin. *Always brush from the unpainted into the freshly painted area.* Use a good brush. For walls and ceilings a four-inch brush is recommended; for woodwork a trim brush.

Dark-colored surfaces may require two coats of Kem-Glo. The second coat may be applied after the first coat has dried for four or five hours. During the painting, if Kem-Glo becomes slightly heavy for brushing it may be thinned with one or two tablespoons of paint thinner or Exolvent, stirred in thoroughly.

Ceilings should be painted first. The Kem-Glo is applied to a strip two or three feet wide, the width of the ceiling. After each few feet it is best to brush lightly crosswise over the freshly painted area to obtain the smoothest finish.

Woodwork should be painted and allowed to dry before the walls are finished with Kem-Glo. The smoothest finish possible will be obtained if the Kem-Glo is applied to several feet of woodwork, after which the brush is drawn across the painted area lightly following the grain of the wood. Kem-Glo should be applied to walls in a strip two or three feet wide, working from ceiling to baseboard. After each few feet we level off the finish by brushing lightly upward into the area previously painted so the finish will be smooth.

On unpainted plaster, two coats of Kem-Glo are applied. No wall primer is needed. Two coats of Kem-Glo are needed on unpainted wood, but no undercoater is necessary. Between coats a light sanding is needed.

Kem-Glo can be intermixed or tinted with Fluid Tinting Colors to produce a large variety of additional pastel tints. It will hold its appearance in luster as well as color, is tough and flexible so that it will stand normal use without cracking or chipping off. Dirt, grime and grease do not penetrate Kem-Glo's plastic-smooth surface. Even ink, fruit juices, beverages, crayon marks and finger prints are all easily removed from a Kem-Glo surface with plain soap and water. Even boiling water will not mar its surface.

There are thousands of possibilities for color combinations with Kem-Glo, Kem-Tone and Kem-Tone Vogue Deep colors. Color can set any mood, for it is a well-known fact that through centuries mankind has developed definite reactions to various colors. The trick is to decide on one predominant color as a foundation on which to build. Then it is high-lighted by using either a color that contrasts or a color that blends—or both.

Super Kem-Tone might be called a superior form of ordinary Kem-Tone and is used in much the same manner as Kem-Tone, although it is available not only for walls and ceilings but for woodwork as well. After three weeks of drying, this finish becomes so hardened that it may be washed time after time without losing any of its beauty. Unlike Kem-Tone, which is thinned by adding 50 per cent of warm water, Super Kem-Tone is used as it comes from the can.

# ( XIX )

## The Ultramodern Finishes

THE functional or modernistic vogue in furniture, homes and shop fittings, such as counters and display cases, has brought with it new demands for different finishes. As a result a series of very beautiful and very simple finishes have been created. They can be produced with materials ordinarily available at moderate cost and there is no reason why, if the following directions are followed, we cannot produce the effects mentioned although occasionally we may have to refer back to our chapter dealing with bleaches.

There are a number of modern finishes that are especially useful in producing "that new look" on functional furniture. These finishes are also practical and in most cases they may be very easily produced.

In the finish about to be outlined, the application of lacquer is preceded by use of bleach, either the type previously described or, in case extreme bleached effects are desired, one of the powerful bleaching mixtures now sold in the large paint stores. They are applied with a rubber sponge, and the worker should use rubber gloves to protect his hands. Most of the powerful new bleaches have hydrogen peroxide in them and no harmful residue is to be found after the bleaching process.

If the worker wishes to check results of these bleaches before he goes "all out," it might be advisable to try the solutions either on test panels or on the underside of the furniture to be finished. It may be said that the results are apt to be disappointing when the finish about to be described is tried on dark walnut or other dark woods. On the other hand, excellent results may be anticipated when it is applied to such woods as maple, birch, chestnut and oak. Pine does not have enough grain character, however, for finishes of this type.

After the wood has thoroughly recovered from the application of the bleach and is completely dry, a mixture of *white* and *clear* lacquer is put on. This mixture is made by adding one part of white lacquer to four parts of clear lacquer. Whether the mixture is sprayed or brushed on the surface, it should be greatly thinned (fifty-fifty) before use. In any event, the wood upon which such a preparation is placed will be greatly lightened and the general effect is apt to be very pleasing. A second or even a third thin coat will not greatly alter the original appearance. It might be mentioned that this is often the finish one sees in many of the smart modernistic shops nowadays. The process itself is referred to as "toning" by modern finishers.

What has become known to the trade as honey-toned maple is also delightful to behold and lies easily within the range of the amateur to produce. White birch may also be treated in the manner reviewed below. To achieve this, the worker simply sands the wood without bleaching it and applies the white and clear lacquer mixture recommended in the previous finish. Over this, two thin coats of water-white lacquer are brushed or sprayed. When these lacquer finishes are brushed on, it may be advisable to use fine waterproof sandpaper between coats.

The so-called honey-tone effect may also be achieved on the above-mentioned woods by the use of the bleaching solution and only the water-white lacquer, which is applied in two or more coats. In this case, the white-clear lacquer mixture is left out.

What has become known as limed oak is also finding wide approval these days. To produce this, the oak is first bleached and then covered with a wash coat of water-white lacquer. Such wash coats are very thin and call for a one-ten mixture (one part lacquer, ten parts thinner) of the water-white lacquer and the thinner. After this has dried, the surface is brushed over with a thinned-out mixture with the consistency of paint, composed of zinc-white oil color and natural color filler. After this has thoroughly dried, one or two applications of water-white lacquer are put on. The end effect should be pleasing.

What has become known as silvered oak is similar to limed oak although the treatment is quite different. In this case, bleaching is followed by the application of a mixture made up of one part of light or pearl gray lacquer and three parts of clear lacquer. One coat of this will be sufficient and, after this has dried, the pores of the grain are filled with white filler thinned out to fluid form. Excess is brushed away with a clean rag moving across the grain. After the latter is absolutely dry and hard, a finishing of two or three thin coats of water-white lacquer is applied after very light sanding.

There is also the bone-white lacquer finish, which is produced in the following manner: Inasmuch as this is not a transparent finish, the use of bleach is not necessary. The worker seeks only a clean, smooth surface. A wash coat of very thin water-white or clear lacquer followed by sanding with No. ooo sandpaper may supply a better base. This is, however, optional.

Bone-white lacquer, which is just off-white, may be already mixed or the worker may produce it himself by adding a touch of brown to white lacquer. The amount of added brown will depend upon the shade desired, but let the mixer beware of the great sensitivity of white lacquer, paint or enamel to the presence of other colors. A few teaspoonfuls of brown to a quart will usually do the trick. Stirring must be complete before the final color can be determined.

The application of bone-white lacquer is followed by a brushed-on application of a medium brown wiping stain which is wiped away before it has a chance to set up. Here the worker may exercise his artistic talents by producing a nice shading effect. These wiping stains are merely concentrated pigment stains.

After the complete drying of the wiping stain, for which at least two days should be allowed, the article is covered with two or more coats of clear lacquer.

This application of a wiping stain and its subsequent removal with a rag is called high-lighting by the trade. Some extremely interesting effects may be obtained with it without a great deal of skill. Perhaps some readers have stopped to admire the "antique maple" effects seen on furniture in the store windows. Such effects are obtained by this high-lighting process. Although such effects are obtained in many different ways, the easiest is that of applying the proper shade of wiping stain and removing most of it. Of course, to wipe the stain away evenly and to leave a uniform color behind would be stupid. On a turned leg, for example, the worker wipes from end to end and makes little attempt to completely remove the stain from grooves. He brushes the rag over the surface in such a manner that only the highest spots are touched. The result is a fine shading. On a paneled cabinet door, he brushes the center clean and leaves the edges with very little or no wiping at all, bleeding off gradually to the edges. If, in the case of "antiqued" maple, a light enough wiping stain has been used, the effect will be perfect. Some practice panels for use with high-lighting will help.

This antique maple effect is produced in the manner described below. In the case of all of these modern finishes it is assumed that fresh, new wood is used. The writer cannot endorse such finishes when it is planned to use them on old wood which may be deeply colored because of age.

The maple or other wood to be finished is first given a coat of red-orange wiping stain. If an error is to be made on the length of time the stain is permitted to remain before it is wiped away, let the error be on the side of too little rather than too much time. As in all cases, a surface that turns out to be too light can be easily remedied, whereas a too-dark surface is a problem indeed. In this first coat of stain, one seeks to produce an even color. High-lighting will follow.

After this stain is completely dry, for which two days should be allowed, the surface should be gone over with a thin coat of clear lacquer. After this has dried, a second coat of wiping stain is placed over the lacquer, and the high-lighting is produced with this. A medium brown stain is used to produce the high-lighting.

When this second application of stain is absolutely dry, the worker proceeds to apply a protective coat of clear lacquer, or even clear varnish if he wishes, remembering that varnish can be placed over lacquer but not lacquer over varnish.

So far in discussing these modern finishes, no mention has been made of mahogany and little mention has been made of walnut.

There are, however, certain modern treatments that may be applied to such woods with pleasing effects.

There is what is known as the "heather" finish for mahogany, the end effects of which vary somewhat with the type of mahogany and its place of growth, Honduras, Cuba, Santo Domingo, etc. In the one case, the mahogany, most of which is a very grainy wood, is filled with a relatively thin mixture of white filler. The excess is wiped away across grain. A very light sanding with No. ooo sandpaper may be advisable after this, working with the grain. An application of two coats of water-white lacquer or varnish follows after long drying.

Another delightful effect referred to in the trade as "tweed" is produced in the manner above, the only change being that of adding a small amount of red color to the natural filler used. This gives a pleasant pink tone.

There are some professional workers who, in some cases, apply a bleach to mahogany and then follow this with a natural-colored filler. This is in turn followed with a diluted stain, the color of which may suit the worker's fancy. Some test panels will reveal the effect most desired. Final covering with water-white lacquer or varnish is recommended.

The same finishes as outlined for mahogany may also be used on walnut if the worker wishes, the final tone varying to some degree. What is known as amber walnut is produced by applying bleach and following this with amber stain. A sealer coat of thin lacquer is then followed by very thin natural filler with a final coat of clear lacquer.

There is still another finish for walnut called "old world." To produce this, the worker first bleaches the wood, using one of the powerful modern preparations. After a seal is produced with a wash coat of very thin clear lacquer, a natural filler tinted with burnt umber is put on. This burnt umber is mixed with oil before being blended with the filler. The depth of tone of this mixture should not be too deep. Much will depend upon the tastes of the worker. Usually a light shade is most desired because shading with a brown wiping stain follows. Finish is produced with clear lacquer or varnish.

If you have a flair for odd effects, you will like the finish outlined below which was developed by the Whitney School for Interior Design in Chicago.

Assuming that the surface has been properly prepared, you paint any light color you wish upon it. Originally two coats of a tangerine color were employed.

After the enamel (Kem-Glo, for example) has set up, you dip a clean small brush into silver paint and strike this brush against a heavy piece of wood carried in the other hand. The brush is moved in the direction of the painted wall before it is suddenly stopped by collision with the wood, whereupon silver paint will leave the brush in specks and spatter the wall. The process is continued until the whole wall or other surface is covered as uniformly as possible. With deeper colors, gold spatter may be used. Of course, this spatter finish is also striking when used upon articles of furniture.

The following finish is intended for close-grained woods. First, we spread a thin coat of flat white or white paint filler over the wood (it is assumed that all preliminary work has been done) and this is wiped off to a thin film that will be transparent. Before this film is dry we apply small amounts of dark blue and vermilion oil colors direct from the tubes, this being applied with a toothbrush. These colors are in turn wiped out with clean rags following the grain. If the film of the white paint has set up too much before we apply the streaks of oil colors, we should moisten the wiping rag with turpentine.

After the job is dry, we can apply several coats of clear varnish with sanding between each coat and a final application of wax.

# ( XX )

# Home Application of Plastic Veneers

WE HAVE all marveled at the perfect woodlike appearance of automobile dashboards and other metallic interior trim used on cars. Many types of wood grain have been beautifully and faithfully simulated by the application of thin plastic films over metal.

Such materials and kits* are now available for home use in the following wood grains: pencil-striped mahogany, prima vera medium, prima vera light, French burl walnut, limed oak, ribbon walnut, riff-cut oak, prima vera mahogany, prima vera gray, African mahogany, cowhide, verd antique marble and breche rose marble.

All these plastic veneers are produced by a photographic process in such a manner that, once applied to furniture, even experts have to examine the surfaces closely before they can be assured that they are not dealing with natural wood.

Once applied, these marvelous films may be lacquered and waxed and are thereafter able to withstand as much abuse as ordinary wood veneers or even more. They are not affected by ordinary wear nor will any of the ordinary alcoholic solvents affect them.

Plastic veneer films (trade name Trans-veneer) are as easily applied as ordinary decalcomanias and no special skill is required. They can be placed over old painted or varnished surfaces and over new wood as well. Thus may the functional, unfinished

* Supplied to paint dealers, hobby shops by Di-Noc Company, 33 Public Square, Cleveland 13, Ohio.

FIG. 23

The left half of this chest is covered with Trans-veneer "limed oak" while the other half was left unfinished for purposes of contrast.

FIG. 24

Trans-veneer "verd antique marble" applied to the wooden top of a modern coffee table. The legs are covered with Trans-veneer "prima vera gray." Such material is alcohol proof.

furniture now available be quickly transformed into articles of great beauty and with every assurance of long life. Once these veneers are properly attached with the kit materials supplied for the purpose, the adhesion produced will defy the years. Full

FIG. 25

The first step in the application of Trans-veneers; cutting the transfers to size.

directions are supplied with each kit, the veneer itself being sold in standard sheet form.

Naturally the more plain the surface to which such veneers are applied the easier the application. Although ordinary curves and corners may be easily covered, it is not recommended that an attempt be made to treat carved surfaces in this manner.

Although not intended for full instructions covering the application of Trans-veneers, the following directions will give us some idea of the simple procedures involved in covering a piece of unfinished furniture.

FIG. 26

After the Trans-veneer is soaked in water for a minute or so and its paper backing is removed, it is laid on the surface to be covered, which has previously been coated with lacquer. A special "welding" coat is then placed beneath the transfer.

First the surfaces are sanded and freed from dust in the manner recommended for the application of enamel. All indentations or old chips should be filled with plastic putty or crack filler and leveled off by sanding. The veneer films are thin enough to reveal such imperfections once the veneer is set in place.

After sanding and removing the dust, the new wood is given a coat of ordinary lacquer sealer. After this is dry and lightly sanded, the work of applying the veneer may begin.

All sheet plastic veneer is protected by a film of paper. There-

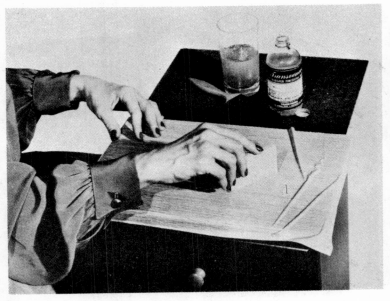

Fig. 27

A rubber squeegee is applied to the Trans-veneer to press out air bubbles and wrinkles. Later, a coat of clear lacquer is brushed over the Trans-veneer, which completes the job.

fore before the plastic veneer is applied to the surface to be treated, it must be soaked in clean warm water long enough to loosen the paper. The paper is not removed until the veneer is carried to the surface to be covered and laid face down with the backing paper on top. Then one half of the veneer is raised and lacquer is applied beneath it. This half is then laid down and the opposite half is raised up and lacquer applied beneath it. After this, the air bubbles are carefully pressed out with a rubber squeegee and the film is left to dry. It is then covered with a coat of lacquer.

FIG. 28

Decorating home-painted furniture with Golden Touch in tape form. Golden Touch is 18-karat gold leaf arranged to be transferred to any surface in the manner of decalcomanias. It is available at paint and hobby stores.

These marvelous and beautiful films may be applied to practically any kind of flat surface including glass, metal and wallboard.

Glastonberry Court
787- 6768

4654
Apt 119